From the Editor

Wide-cut rug hooking is enjoying unprecedented growth in the fiber arts world. That may be due to the time element involved—wide-cut projects can be completed quicker than fine-cut projects. But undoubtedly, rug hookers have found ways to incorporate the look of fine-cut shading with creative dyeing techniques.

Hooked rugs were considered to be America's one indigenous folk art. Rug Hooking first appeared in the eighteen century in Atlantic Canada and New England. At that time, it was considered to be a craft of poverty. Our predecessors used any materials they had on hand—old clothing, blankets, feed sacks—to create rugs to cover their bare floors. Most designs were disregarded. These charming rugs of yesteryear still have appeal today and reflect life in a simpler time.

Whatever draws you to the wide-cut look, hooking and completing a small project is appealing. Accomplishing a finished piece of work such as a purse, pillow, or tablemat is fun to do and provides an immediate feeling of accomplishment. Today's rug hookers have gone beyond making strictly utilitarian floor coverings to also making small projects such as door pockets, runners, pillows, tea cozies, and more.

Each article in *Pattern Designs for Rug Hookers* contains a materials list, hooking and finishing instructions, a pattern line drawing, designer's tips, and contact information about the artist.

For a good look at what rug hookers are doing with yesteryear's craft, pick up a copy of *Rug Hooking* magazine or visit our web site at *www.rughookingmagazine.com.* Within the world of rug hooking and *Rug Hooking* magazine, you'll find a style to suit every taste and a growing community of giving, gracious fiber artists who will welcome you to their gatherings.—*Ginny Stimmel*

D1567485

Pattern Designs for Rug Hookers

Editor
Virginia P. Stimmel

Book Designer
CW Design Solutions, Inc.

Photographer
Impact Xpozures

Advertising Coordinator
Dana Monlish

Chairman
M. David Detweiler

Operations Manager
Anne Lodge-Smith

Presented by

R·U·G HOOKING

5067 Ritter Road
Mechanicsburg, PA 17055
(717) 796-0411
(800) 732-3669

www.rughookingmagazine.com
rughook@
stackpolebooks.com

PRINTED IN USA
Contents Copyright© 2009. All rights reserved. Reproduction in whole or in part without the written consent of the publisher is prohibited.

ISBN: 1-881982-69-6;

978-1-881982-69-2

Table of Contents

From the Editor 1

About the Magazine 3

Abundance 4
by Cherylyn Brubaker/Hooked Treasures

Bird Rug 11
by Maria Barton/Star Rug Company

Botanical Garden Sampler 16
by Tina Payton/Payton Primitives

Calico Cat Pillow 22
by Jill Holmes/Northwoods Wool

Fowl Mood 26
by Gene Shepherd

My Primitive Tulip 32
by Lois Roy/Olde Scotties Primtives

**Peaceful Garden,
Hooked Door Pocket** 37
by Sharon Soule/Crow Hill Primitives

Sheep Sampler 42
by Wendy Barton Miller/The Red Saltbox

**Sheep's in the Meadow
Footstool** 48
by Connie Litfin and Marti Taylor/Mustard Seed Primitives

Sherman 54
by Jeanne Field with Lois Reesor/Rittermere-Hurst-Field

Snow Day 60
by Shelley Flannery and Barbara A. Hanson/Threads of Comfort Designs

Tulip Basket Runner 66
by Karen Worthington/The Blue Tulip

Under the Willow 70
by Kris Miller/Spruce Ridge Studios

Very Veggie Runner 76
by Martha Reeder and Liz Quebe/GoingGray

Wooly Saltbox Cozy 81
by Kim Kowula/Prim N Proper Stitches

General Rug Hooking Instructions 86

Resources 88

About The Magazine

Our Beginnings

In the 150 years since rug hooking made its way to North America, no periodicals covered the subject until professional rug designer Joan Moshimer began publishing *Rug Hooker News & Views* in 1972, a newsletter "by and for rug hookers." But as more people took up the craft and the rug hooking industry flourished, it became apparent that only a full-fledged magazine could best serve the growing audience.

In 1989, Stackpole Inc., a Pennsylvania-based book and magazine publisher, transformed Joan's newsletter into *Rug Hooking*, the only full-color, internationally read magazine devoted exclusively to the subject of hand-hooked rugs.

Rug Hooking Magazine

Rug Hooking brings its readers striking color photographs of gorgeous rugs and stories that both inspire and instruct. Each issue of *Rug Hooking* contains articles on dyeing, color planning, designing, hooking techniques, rug hooking history, and more. Feature articles cover topics ranging from elaborate Orientals to country-style primitives.

Books From *Rug Hooking*

In addition to publishing five issues of the magazine each year, *Rug Hooking* also publishes books, of which *Celebration of Hand-Hooked Rugs* is one. Through the years *Celebration* has brought hundreds of beautiful rugs to the attention of rug hookers worldwide.

The Framework Series was introduced in 1998. Books in this series include: *People and Places: Roslyn Logsdon's Imagery in Fiber.* Other books include *Preserving the Past in Primitive Rugs* by designer Barbara Brown; *A Rug Hooker's Garden,* in which 10 experts teach how to hook a bouquet of blossoms; *Hooked on the Wild Side* by Elizabeth Black, a recognized expert on hooking animals, both domestic and wild; *The Rug Hooker's Bible* by Jane Olson and Gene Shepherd, based on 30 years of *The Rugger's Roundtable* newsletter; *Designs for Primitive Hookers* by Jenny Rupp and Lisa Yeago, featuring 19 projects and patterns; *Sculpted Rugs in Waldoboro Style* by Jacqueline Hansen with Trudy Brown; *Creating an Antique Look in Hand-Hooked Rugs* by Cynthia S. Norwood; *Prodded Hooking for a Three-Dimensional Effect* by Gene Shepherd; and *Hooked Rug Landscapes* by Anne-Marie Littenberg.

Our other books include *Basic Rug Hooking,* a compilation of 12 beginner's projects and directions on design, color planning, wool selection, and hooking techniques, plus exclusive pull-out patterns; *The Secrets of Primitive Hooked Rugs* by Barbara Carroll, who takes you step-by-step through the process of creating a full-sized Wooly Horse pattern; *The Secrets of Color in Hand-Hooked Rugs* by Betty Krull, an expert on color-planning and color theory; and *The Secrets of Planning and Designing Hand-Hooked Rugs* by Deanne Fitzpatrick, a well-known Canadian author on rug hooking and a member of our Editorial Board; and *Rug Hooking 20th Anniversary 2008.*

Books and magazines aren't the only way we communicate with the rug hooking community. Our web site (*www.rughookingmagazine.com*) is packed with vivid photos, informative text, and links to other helpful sites. For more information on *Rug Hooking* magazine and its other publications, write to 5067 Ritter Road, Mechanicsburg, PA 17055 or call (800) 732-3669.

Abundance

by Cherylyn Brubaker/Hooked Treasures

A little challenging but well worth the effort, *Abundance* is a fun pattern that will cheer up any room. You can choose to render the fruit realistically or in a more primitive, flat fashion. Since produce typically has very distinctive colors, the challenge is using the color in quantities that will pull the color plan together. I will admit to changing some of the fruit to other varieties in order to move the color across the pattern.

This bright color palette is unusual for me, but after what seemed to be a never-ending long Maine winter, I needed color. One of my favorite rugs has a soft yellow background. After making a background color selection everything else fell into place.

As you look at the list of materials don't be put off. Because I tried to make the produce look somewhat lifelike, different values of colors were necessary. Many of the fabrics are small pieces and you just may have what you need left over from a previous project.

Transferring the Pattern

The finished rug size is 19" x 30". You will need a piece of backing with about 4"-5" extra on each side to work comfortably. The artwork should be enlarged 343% to be full sized. I find that bleached primitive linen can be laid over a good dark drawing and traced without the use of Red Dot Tracer cloth. If you are using monk's cloth you will either need a light table, well-lit window or pattern tracing cloth. To prevent color transfer to your wool, please use an industrial marker and never a color other than black. Be sure to secure the edge either by sewing or with masking tape to prevent further raveling.

Getting Started

Choose the background color and from there do your other color planning. Because color changes, depending on what it sits next to, this is crucial. For example, I knew that using the warm gold in the background meant that the pear in the compote had to be a greener, sharper yellow, or a different variety of pear altogether for it to stand out. The sharp green/yellow color is central and eye-catching. To move that color somewhere else, I chose to hook the tangerine in the lower right with a definite yellow cast and also used the same pungent yellow in the flower centers.

In this project, hooking direction is important as well. The round fruit was not hooked in a bull's eye fashion. Hooking a skeletal framework and then filling in gives these forms a more realistic look.

I hooked this mat using a #7 cut except for the strawberries and their leaves and stems. The stems are hooked with a #5 while the leaves and berries are cut in #6. The delicate leaves would have lost their shape if they had been hooked in a wider cut. There is probably no reason why a #8 cut would not work for the background. However, if you are working with multi-cuts, pick a median height to work in.

Abundance, 30" x 19", #5-, 6-, and 7-cut wool on primitive linen. Designed and hooked by Cherylyn Brubaker of Hooked Treasures, Brunswick, Maine, 2009.

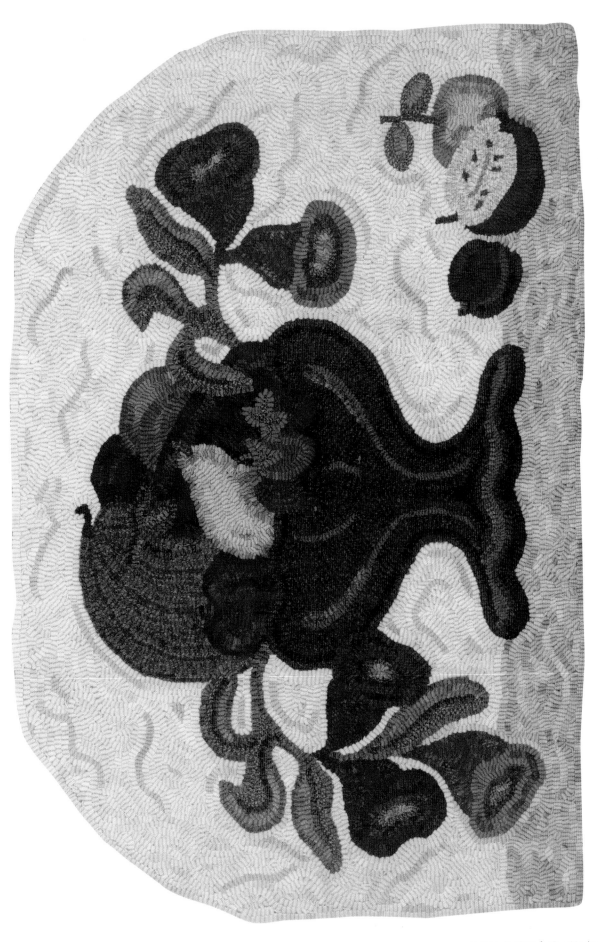

- Foundation monk's cloth or linen 29" x 40"

Wool Fabric
*All cut in #7 with the exception of the strawberries. These colors repeat in other motifs; that's why the list is long.

Compote
Forest Greens (4 values)
- Medium heather–18" x 17"
- Dark blue spruce–8" x 16"
- Light green plaid–2" x 18"
- Light green stripe– 4" x 17¹/₂"

Strawberries #6 Cut
- Bright red–2" x 16"
- Light red–2" x 17"
- Red plaid–5" x 16¹/₂"
- Orange red–2" x 16"

Strawberry Leaves #6 Cut
- Bright green solid–2" x 16" (outline)
- Blue green herringbone– 3" x 16"

Strawberry Stems #5 Cut
- Green plaid–a few strands

Pear (2 values)
- Acid yellow solid–2" x 17"
- Yellow/green plaid–7¹/₂" x 16"
- Dark gold hound's-tooth– 1 strand

Eggplant (3 values)
- Bright purple–6" x 16"
- Plum–4" x 17"
- Dark grape–3" x 17"

Eggplant Stem/Leaves
- Blue/green plaid–10" x 16"
- Bright green texture– 9" x 16¹/₂"

Apple (3 values)
- Red plaid (fromStrawberries)
- Red spot dye–3" x 16"
- Dark red texture–2" x 16"
- Light red for highlight–a few strands

Melon
- Brown/green/gold plaid– 14" x 16"
- Green/brown–1 strand for stem

Peach
- Rusty red–3" x 16"
- Dip dye rust to gold–2¹/₂" x 16"

Red Plum (3 values)
- Rose red hound's tooth– 4" x 16"
- Red purple heather–3" x 17"
- Dark wine herringbone– 3" x 16"

Left and Right Side Leaves
- Yellow green herringbone– 4" x 17"
- Moss green–4" x 16¹/₂"
- Bright green texture (from eggplant)
- Blue/green plaid (from eggplant)

Flowers (Rose Red/ Orange Combo)
- Rose red hound's-tooth (from Red Plum)
- Plaid multi–6" x 17"
- Orange–3" x 16"
- Brown plaid–2" x 17"
- Blue/green herringbone (from Strawberry Leaves)
- Yellow/green plaid (from Pear)

Flowers (Red/Purple Combo)
- Red plaid (from Strawberries)
- Orange/red (from Strawberries)
- Purples (from Eggplant)
- Brown plaid (from Flower above)
- Blue/green herringbone (from Strawberry Leaves)
- Yellow/green plaid (from Pear)

Cut Apple
- Rough light gold texture– 2¹/₂" x 16"
- Brown plaid (from Flowers)
- 2 darkest reds (from Apple)
- Stem (same as Melon)–1 strand

Purple Plum
- 3 purples (from Eggplant)
- Tangerine:
- Orange (from Flower)
- Acid yellow solid (from Pear)
- Yellow/green plaid (from Pear)
- Rust to gold dip dye (from Peach)

Tangerine Leaves
- Yellow green herringbone (from Leaves above)
- Moss green (from Leaves above)
- Stem - brown texture–1 strand

Background Light to Dark
- Light gold spot dye–19" x 56"
- Solid light gold–4" x 17"
- Gold/green spot dye–8" x 16"
- Gold/tan spot dye– 14" x 18¹/₂"
- Medium yellow–3" x 16"

Edging
- Complimentary fabric–5" x 60"

Line drawing used for **Abundance**.
Enlarge to 19" x 30" (343%).

Hooking the Design

I started *Abundance* by hooking the compote. I chose a grouping of forest greens knowing that I would want to use vibrant yellow greens for the leaves. The main green used is a heathered fabric that was a recycled pant leg. I hooked the compote outline with this fabric but used the darker blue spruce for the bottom two rows along the base. The second line in on the sides and along the top is also that blue spruce fabric. From there the heather is used for most of the compote except for the highlights. The highlights are merely contour lines that mimic the shape of the vase. These are the two lighter shades. The dark area at the center of the base is filled in with the blue spruce wool and is formed by those contour lines. The darkest wool is hooked under the berries to create a shadow. I found it quite helpful to hook holding lines throughout, where motifs overlapped but had not been hooked in yet.

The strawberries should be hooked in conjunction with the compote because they overlap. As with all the produce in the compote, hook the closest objects first and proceed back in the space. The strawberry leaves are outlined with the bright green solid and filled with the blue green herringbone. Choose your lightest red for the closest berry and darker reds for the ones behind.

The pear is hooked using at least two values of yellow. For mine, I had a Pendleton shirt plaid that was an acid yellow/green plaid. Various parts of the plaid were lighter and darker. The pear was outlined using the darker part of the plaid with one strand of dark gold hound's-tooth hooked where the pear touches the strawberries. The yellow solid was hooked where the pear was lightest.

The eggplant is darkest where it sits against the strawberries. Hook your darkest purple value there. Decide where the highlight is and put that in using the lightest value. I used the bright purple for most of the eggplant. The green top is outlined with the blue/green plaid and filled with a bright green texture.

Next up is the apple. I chose to use the darkest reds along the edges. Decide where you want your highlights and remember to hook a skeletal frame. You can even draw these lines in. Take care to make sure that the reds of the apple show up against the melon fabric.

For the melon I found a perfect brown plaid. By separating the brown lines of the plaid I was able to create the ribbing in the melon. Inside the brown lines the plaid pieces with yellow and green were quieter and worked well. The stem is one strand of green/brown hound's-tooth.

Hooking the peach is not too difficult. A rusty red combined with selected pieces of the dip dyed rust to gold create the two lobes of the peach shape.

There isn't too much of the plum showing in the compote. Because the eggplant is purple, I decided to hook a redder plum. Place the highlights near the top. Where the plum sits against the peach, melon and eggplant use the darkest wool. The red purple heather fills the rest of the fruit.

The leaves on either side of the compote are hooked using four yellow/green wools. They are outlined with the bright green texture used in the eggplant stem. The veins are the blue/green plaid (also from the eggplant). One side of each leaf is filled with the yellow/green herringbone and the other side with moss green.

Two flower color combinations serve to move the color from the fruit down. Three flowers are red/purple and two are rose red/orange. You'll notice that all the flower centers are the same combination of three colors—a brown plaid, the blue green herringbone from the strawberry leaves, and the pear yellow/green plaid. This helps to unify them. Also, one of the three red/purple flowers is slightly different. The two purples in the ruffle are reversed. The rose red/orange flowers have accents from a snazzy multi plaid in them just for fun. This completes the fruit compote. There are only three more pieces of fruit remaining until you're an expert!

The purple plum is hooked using the three

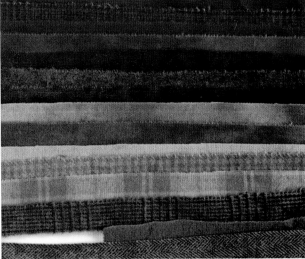

Wool samples used for hooking **Abundance**.

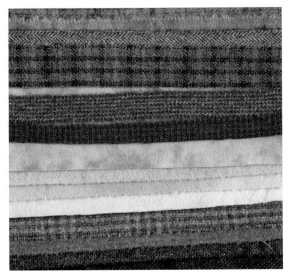

purples from the eggplant. The darkest shade works well at the outer edges. Put in a highlight and surround with the medium purple. The stem is the blue/green plaid from the leaf veins.

I thought the cut apple would be the most problematic fruit because of the lightness of the flesh. However, the rough light gold texture worked with the background. The seeds are the same brown plaid from the flower centers. The red apple skin is derived from the two darkest values used in the apple above. The color of the stem is the same green/brown hound's-tooth as the melon's stem.

Adding the yellow from the pear into the tangerine can be a little tricky because orange

is necessary on the outer edge to work with the background gold. Also, too much yellow near the apple flesh won't work either. I found that selected strips of the peach's rust to gold dip dye and darker strands from the Pendleton yellow/green plaid helped with the transition. A random piece of brown texture makes a suitable stem. The leaves are simply outlined with the yellow green herringbone and filled with the moss green.

All that remains is the background. I usually never leave it all to do in the end. However, when creating a horizontal plane the objects sitting above need to be completed. If working the background in one fabric or value it is easily worked on at the same time as the motifs are

Cherylyn Brubaker

A former graphic designer with a Bachelor of Fine Arts from the University of Connecticut, Cherylyn Brubaker now owns Hooked Treasures, a rug hooking business where she also offers classes most of the year. Her rug hooking addiction began in 1995 when a friend was taking lessons. Cherylyn joined her friend's class and has created more than 50 pieces, including wall hangings and pillows. She is certified with the Rug Hooking Guild of Nova Scotia's Teachers Branch and also teaches at various camps and rug hooking guilds. For further information on Cherylyn's patterns, visit her web site at www.hookedtreasures. com, (207) 729-1380.

filled in. On my rug all of the background hooking was completed at once. The darker spot dyed wools were combined and hooked randomly in a mostly horizontal fashion at the base of the compote and under the three pieces of fruit. From there I worked upward with the lighter wool, randomly hooking in strips of the gold/tan spot dye and a solid gold piece.

Finishing the Rug

Look over your rug for places you have missed or holidays. I chose to finish my rug with a wool fabric edging. You can hand sew it closely to the hooked edge, after lightly steaming the mat, or machine sew it on as a facing well before the background hooking is done. To do this, simply tear a 2¹/₂" piece lengthwise and piece additional yardage until it is long enough to wrap around

the rug circumference. If machine sewing, it is applied wrong side out along the pattern edge to be folded over after the hooking is completed. A zigzag should be sewn about 1" away from the pattern edge to prevent fraying after the excess is cut away. Fold the binding to the reverse side and hand-sew folding the rough edge of the wool binding under. Give the mat a good steaming loop side down with an iron and a damp cloth. Lay flat on a towel until completely dry.

NOTE: *This pattern and all others shown in this book can be ordered through the* **Rug Hooking** *magazine web site at www. rughookingmagazine.com.*

Bird Rug

by Maria Barton/Star Rug Company

One of my favorite motifs to hook is a bird and you will find them in many of the rugs that I hook and design. Birds work well in primitive rug hooking because they look great no matter what their color. For this pattern, I planned on making the bird the focus of the pattern by making it large, but I started drawing some of the flower motifs and they became an integral part of this design.

Transferring the Pattern

To enlarge the pattern, take it to a copy store and ask them to enlarge it by 250%. The finished size of my rug is 20" x 25$\frac{1}{2}$". After you have enlarged the pattern, draw the pattern on the backing using the transfer method of your choice. To use Red Dot Tracer, place the Red Dot fabric over the pattern and trace with a black marker. Next, place the Red Dot onto your foundation piece and trace over the Red Dot pattern with a black magic maker thereby bleeding the pattern onto the foundation piece. You could also use a light table to transfer the pattern. When transferring the pattern, make sure that the outside lines of the pattern are straight on the grain.

Prior to hooking, sew a zigzag stitch or serge around the edge of your foundation to prevent raveling during hooking. Leave at least 4" around the pattern so that it will fit onto your rug hooking frame or hoop.

Attaching the Binding Prior to Hooking

Prior to hooking the rug, I sew my binding tape onto the pattern. If you sew the tape onto the pattern before you hook, you can use a sewing machine to attach it to the foundation. If you wait until the rug is hooked, it is better to sew the binding by hand. I've only recently started binding using this method and it saves me an hour or two depending on the size of the rug.

To sew the binding prior to hooking, place the binding tape on the outside line of the pattern and begin sewing. Stitch the binding tape onto the foundation close to the edge of the design. Sewing the binding around the corners can be a little tricky but if you manipulate the binding by holding it and turning it at the corner and moving the sewing machine slowly, you will be able to do it. To finish attaching the binding tape, turn the binding tape under and place it over the attached binding (where you began sewing the binding onto the foundation). Sew it over the binding about $\frac{1}{2}$". This provides for a nice clean finish to the binding.

Flowers

When hooking the flower motifs, I used #8 cut strips of wool. Smaller motifs can sometimes be tricky to hook and often definition is lost if not hooked correctly. When hooking smaller motifs like these flowers, hook them with the wool of your choice. Next, hook around the flower using your background wool by hooking the wool closely (packed) around the flowers. Make sure that you hook nearly every hole around the flower. Packing the wool helps

Bird Rug, 25$\frac{1}{2}$" x 20", #8-cut wool on primitive linen. Designed and hooked by Maria Barton, Indian River, Michigan, 2009.

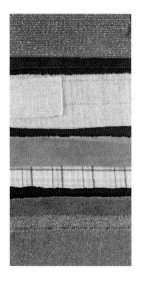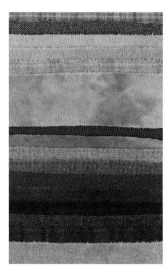

Wool samples used for the **Bird Rug**.

to give small motifs with intricate details definition. If the wool were not packed, you would lose the shape of the flower. Keep in mind, the only time to pack wool is around small motifs or motifs requiring more definition and detail like the flowers. Hook all the flowers using this technique.

Have fun with the flowers. The flowers offer the opportunity to introduce a lot of color and personality into the rug. As you can see, I chose bold colors, which provide quite a contrast with the neutral colored wool. This design would look wonderful with primitive colors as well. Try a dark background and hook all the flowers in different primitive colors like mustard, pumpkin, cranberry, blue, and green. Hook the bird in a nice neutral color.

Bird

If you are like me, you have accumulated hundreds of strips of wool from your rug hooking projects. You can use some of those strips in this pattern. Try separating your strips into groups of similar color values and hook the bird using the wool from that color group. This is what I did for the bird using the wool from my pile of blue strips of wool. Hooking a motif using this method provides for much more depth than using just one piece of wool. You could also try hooking some other colors of wool into the bird. If you look closely at my bird, I have used green wool. Maybe try some strips of orange if you are

hooking a yellow bird or purple strips of wool in a red bird. The bird is such a large motif that you don't want to hook it simply with one piece of wool. You could have some fun with the bird and hook the wing with different strips of wool in a hit or miss fashion. Or try hooking different sections of the bird in different directions. Part of the bird could be hooked horizontally and the other part vertically. Maybe you could embellish the bird's wing with buttons. The bird is so big that it provides the perfect opportunity to be a little creative. Have fun with the bird!

Materials List

- 30" x 41" piece of primitive linen
- Black permanent marker
- 3 yards of black binding tape
- Red Dot Tracer or light box

Wool:

- Background–2 yards of neutral
- Flowers–1/8 yard each of different shades of pink and red
- Bird–½ yard blue
- Border–¼ yard each of red and pink

Line drawing used for **Bird Rug**. Enlarge to 25½" x 20" (250%).

Background

For the background, I used two different neutral colored wools (#9 cut) that had some texture in them to hook around the flowers and bird. The texture in the wool helps the background from looking flat. However, you could try the technique described earlier (gather wool strips in similar values) and use this wool to hook the background.

Border

Because the rug design is busy, keep the border simple by hooking several rows of wool around the rug. Pull colors from either the flowers or the bird to hook the border. My border is small with only two strips but you could hook 5 to 10 rows around the rug to give the appearance of a frame.

Finishing the Rug

After the pattern is hooked, either serge or zigzag around the pattern about ½" from the edge of the rug. If you pre-attached your binding, be careful not to catch it in the serger or sewing machine. If zigzagged cut away the excess foundation. Before steaming the rug, take the time to remove excess wool dust from your rug before steaming it. You can use either a lint brush or an attachment to a sweeper. Roll the lint brush or sweep all over the front of your rug. This is an important step as that ever-pesky wool dust gathers on your hooked piece as you hook. You'll be amazed at the amount of dust that you will pick up from your hooked surface.

The next step is to steam your rug. Place a protective cloth over the pad of your ironing board and lay the hooked side face down. Place a damp cloth over the back of the rug and place the iron on the rug, hold and steam. Move the iron to the next area and steam. Continue in this fashion until the entire surface has been steamed. Turn the rug over and press the front of the rug using the same method. Press the excess foundation to the back of the hooked piece. Lay the piece flat and allow it to dry overnight. If you attached your binding to the rug before hooking, you should blind stitch the binding to the back of your rug. Otherwise, you will need to attach the binding to the rug using the technique of choice.

Remember to add a tag to the back of your rug with your name, year hooked and any other details you'd like to provide about the rug. You can make a simple tag by writing with a permanent marker the information onto a piece of muslin and sewing it to the back of the rug.

NOTE: **This pattern and all others shown in this book can be ordered through the Rug Hooking** *magazine web site at* **www. rughookingmagazine.com.**

Maria Barton

Maria lives in Northern Michigan and has been hooking rugs since 1992. She is best known for her whimsical, primitive style and enjoys designing Halloween-themed rugs. Early American Life has twice recognized her as a top artisan for her reproduction style rugs. Maria writes articles for Rug Hooking *magazine and other publications. For further information on Maria's rugs contact her at* starrugcompany@free way.net, *231-238-6894,* www.starrugcompany.com.

Botanical Garden Sampler

by Tina Payton/Payton Primitives

Living in the Western Mountains of Maine, the winter months can be long and hard. Like so many other Mainers, I look forward to, and enjoy, the sites and signs of, springtime. I am once again reminded of how hard and harsh the Maine winter season is as it destroyed my Bee Balm and Cone Flowers. These blossoms have been a longtime favorite in my garden.

I've thought for sometime now, that I needed to design a botanical sampler, which would include some of these favorites. With this in mind, I designed *Botanical Garden Sampler*. Although this is a primitive design, it could very easily be hooked in a more traditional manner, using smaller cuts and more detailed shading. I've selected somewhat vibrant colors for the flowers, and by encompassing them with subtle, muted tones, I'm able to achieve the primitive look I love.

Enlarging and Transferring the Design

To begin, you will need to enlarge the pattern. Most copy centers can easily accommodate this type of an enlargement. This pattern is designed to be enlarged by 351%, or until the design measures 16" x 36". Choose the foundation material of your choice, remembering to allow 3-4" of extra linen on all sides. I recommend using bleached Dorr linen, which allows you to lay your linen over the pattern without requiring the use of a light box or red dot paper.

Before you start transferring your design to linen, you will want to determine the center. A simple and effective way to do this is to fold the linen in half length-wise, and then in half width-wise, using your finger as a guide to press a good crease as you go. When you unfold the linen, the center will easily be visible.

To ensure that your lines are perfectly straight on the grain, rather than drawing it from the pattern directly, I recommend that you do the following using a tape measure. Measure and place a mark 18" on each side of your center, horizontally, and 8" on each side of your center, vertically. Using a permanent marker and following your marks, hold your permanent marker straight up within the groove of the grain. Pull the permanent marker to create a rectangle measuring 16" x 36". Using a tape measure, measure in 2" from the outside lines. Repeat the same steps previously described. This will create your borderlines. Once all outlines have been completed, place the linen on top of the paper pattern and trace inside motifs, outlines and border ribbon. To prevent fraying, surge all edges or zigzag two rows around all edges.

Cutting Widths

Botanical Garden Sampler is a fairly quick rug to hook. The flowers, stems, and all leaves are done using a #7 cut. An #8½ cut was used for both the background and the border.

Botanical Garden Sampler, 36" x 16", #7- and #8½-cut wool on linen. Designed and hooked by Tina Payton, Mexico, Maine, 2009.

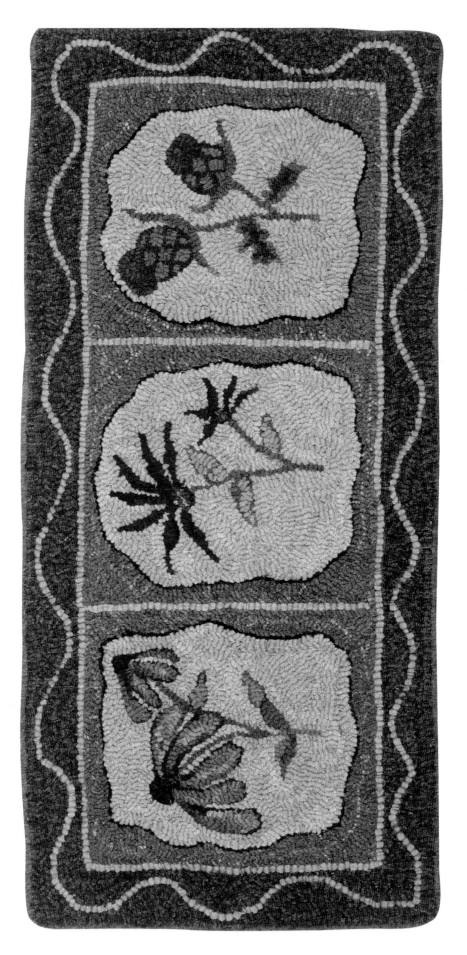

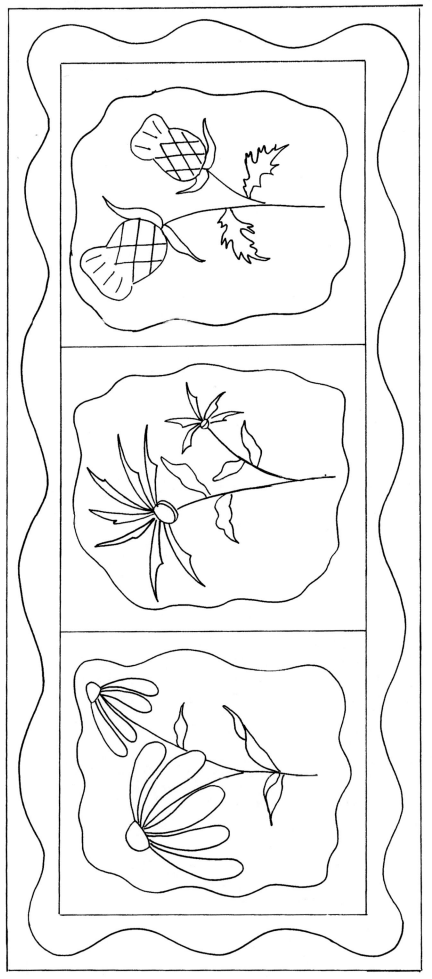

Line drawing used for **Botanical Garden Sampler.** Enlarge to 16" x 36" (351%).

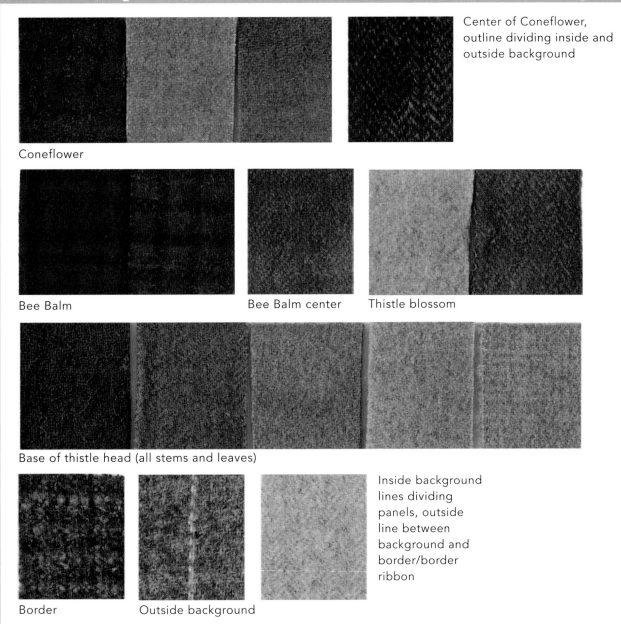

Center of Coneflower, outline dividing inside and outside background

Coneflower

Bee Balm

Bee Balm center

Thistle blossom

Base of thistle head (all stems and leaves)

Inside background lines dividing panels, outside line between background and border/border ribbon

Border

Outside background

Hooking

To give it movement, contour hooking is used to fill in the motifs and background. This is similar to echo quilting, where the quilter follows the shapes of the motifs, echoing outward.

Be sure to stay within the lines of your motifs to prevent your design from becoming enlarged. Quite often when outlining my motifs, I prefer to use a thin outline rather than a wider, more bold outline. This is the case with the petals and leaves of the flowers, as well as the outline separating the inner background from the outer background. Using a #3 cut, you will want to outline these areas by hooking into the same holes originally hooked to create the design. Keep in mind, even though the #3 cut is much smaller, you will need to pull your loops up evenly with the others.

Materials List

- Foundation of your choice
- Coneflower–$1/3$ yard over dyed various dark, medium and light valued pinks and mauves
- Bee balm–$1/8$ yard over dyed various reds
- Bee balm center–2" gold
- Thistle base, all flowers stems and leaves–$5/8$ yard various over dyed greens
- Thistle flowering head–5" over dyed purple
- Inner background around all three flowers, dividing lines between each panel, frame line around rug, which separates the inner background from the border, and the ribbon flowing through the border–$1 5/8$ yards over dyed textured beige
- Outer background–½ yard textured tan
- Border–¾ yards as is plaid green
- Center of cone flower–outline between inside background and outer background–6" over dyed dark brown wool in #3 cut

Finishing Materials:

- Binding tape
- $1/4$" cotton cording
- Rug weight yarn

- Large eyed needle
- Standard needle
- Thread

After you have completed all hooking of your rug, check for ends that may need trimmed. Turn your rug over and check for any spots that may require additional hooking. When you are satisfied you have completed all hooking, use a damp towel to press the backside of your rug. Continue wetting your towel and steam pressing several times. If your rug needs squared up a bit, this is the time to shape it. Lay your rug on a towel and allow it to dry.

Binding

There are several different methods to binding a rug. For this project, I chose to whip stitch my rug with wool yarn.

Before beginning, you should wash and dry your binding tape. To determine the length of binding you will need, measure around all sides of your rug. Add an additional 3" per yard, to allow for shrinkage.

On all four sides, measure and mark approximately 3" out from your last row of

hooking. Using the marks as your guide, once again, place your Sharpie marker in the grooves and pull, creating what will now be your cutting guide. Surge or zigzag two rows around the edge of your foundation. You will be folding this remaining foundation over your cotton cording. Using a tape measure, measure around your finished rug to determine the total length of cording that you will need to make it around all four sides. Add an additional 4-6" to the cording. This will allow for ease in joining your two ends. Starting on any side, place the cording on the backside of your work, turning your 3" foundation over the cording. Next, sew a running stitch around the entire rug, forming a casing around the cording. Once you have made it around your entire rug, cut the cording so the two ends meet and whip stitch them together. When creating your casing, it is not necessary to make small stitches, you're only holding your cording in place to make it easier to wrap. Cut a generous length of wool yarn to work with. I generally use about 3' at a time. (Anything longer than this tends to get tangled.) A good rule of thumb is to start your whipping anywhere other than a corner. Place your completed rug wrong side up in front of you. Begin your whipping by inserting your needle from the back to the front. I'm right handed so I whip as I hook, from left to right. If you are left handed, you may want to whip in the opposite direction. By whipping from the back to the front, your whipped edge turns toward the back of your rug rather than the front, showing less of your whipping and framing your piece nicely. Beginning by leaving a tail a couple inches long, insert your needle as close to your hooked work as possible, while wrapping your wool yarn completely around your cording and reinserting your needle next to your previous insertion point. Pay special care in catching and covering your tail as you go. Keep your wrapping close together to prevent your foundation from showing through. You will want it to be snug but not so tight that it causes your rug to bunch and not lay flat. When you have reached the end of the length of yarn, you will want to leave a couple of inches to be hidden under your previous whipped cording. This will prevent your whipping from unraveling. To do this, simply run your needle under your previously wrapped section, pulling snugly and clip. Repeat this process until you have completed wrapping your rug.

Once this is complete, you will need to sew your binding tape to the back of the rug. This will cover any excess foundation. Lay your binding flat and up against your wrapped cording. Beginning in about 2" from the end of your binding, begin sewing your binding. I like my rug to have a neat finish to it. In order to accomplish this, I recommend using a blind stitch. Begin by inserting your needle into the foundation and coming up and just catching the edge of your binding tape. Insert your needle into the foundation, directly beside where your thread came through. Run your needle under the binding about ¼" to ½" away, coming back up through the edge of the binding. Once again, insert your needle into your foundation directly next to where your needle came through the binding. Continue in this manner until you have made it back around to the beginning of your rug. (If you have done this correctly, you will only see where you caught the edge of your binding.) Trim your ends so that you have about an inch overlapping the start of your binding tape. Fold both ends under and stitch in place. Repeat this process for the other side of your binding tape.

Labels

Don't forget to make your label for the back of your rug. Put as much detail as you can. Remember, your rug will be an heirloom one day and the more information you have on it, the better. If it's a special gift for someone's birthday, mark it on your tag. Be sure to document who the designer was, who hooked it, the date, etc.

NOTE: *This pattern and all others shown in this book can be ordered through the* **Rug Hooking** *magazine web site at* www. rughookingmagazine.com.

Tina Payton

Tina has been designing, selling and teaching various forms of art for over 25 years. Her love of art started as a young child when she enrolled in an art program at the local community center. In 1997 she was introduced to rug hooking. By 2005 she began teaching classes and soon developed her web site, www. paytonprimitives.com, *(207) 364-2172. Tina's hooked rug designs have been incorporated into floorcloths, penny rugs, and needle punch including* Botanical Garden, *which is available through* Rug Hooking *magazine as a hooked rug design.*

Calico Cat Pillow

by Jill Holmes/Northwoods Wool

This cat pillow is a quick project and a wonderful tribute to all of the annoying, noisy, fur shedding, bird chasing, and wonderful cats in the world!

Transferring the Pattern

Begin by enlarging the cat pattern by 140% to 14" x 10". Using a light box, netting or Red Dot Tracer, transfer the pattern to your monk's cloth. Use a Sharpie or some other permanent marker when drawing your pattern. It is important to place the bottom of the cat on the straight of the grain of the monk's cloth. Leave at least 4" of extra cloth around the cat to make sure the pattern will fit on your frame.

About the Wool

The wool that was used for this project is a mix of textured pieces and a mottled solid. Textured wool is so wonderful to work with. It lends life and interest to all hooked pieces and it camouflages difficult hooked areas. The cat's black and orange patches are both textured and the light areas are a white piece mottled with a gray/brown.

Hooking the Pattern

When hooking this pattern it is best to use #6 cut strips for the face and paws while using #7s or #8s for the body. The entire cat is outlined with solid antique black wool using the strip sizes recommended previously—#6s for the face and paws and #7s for the rest of the body.

1. Begin hooking the cat by outlining the face using #6 cut black strips.
2. Narrow a #6 strip by cutting it in half lengthwise. Use this strip to outline the eyes and to hook the bridge of the nose. The actual nose and mouth are hooked with the #6 black strips. Hook inside the nose outline as much as possible or you will end up with a big blob for a nose (experience speaking here).
3. To fill in the eyes you need to hook the pupils first. Using a #6 cut black strip begin at the top center of the cat's eyes. Hook two loops going toward the bottom of the eye. The next step is to hook the colored part of the eye. Do this by hooking a U around the black loops that you just put in. Use a #6 cut green or gold strip for this part. To fill in the corners of the eyes, use #6 strips of white wool.
4. Following your pattern lines and referring to the picture of the pillow, hook the remainder of the cat's face. The "whisker dots" and the whiskers will be done later on.
5. Now outline the entire body of the cat and the tail using the wider strips of antique black.
6. Next, the paws can be hooked. Outline them using the #6 cut strips of black and hook the toe lines with the same strips. Fill in the paws with #6 cut orange strips.
7. Once again referring to the picture and using the lines on the pattern, fill in the cat's body.

Calico Cat Pillow, 14" x 10", #6-, 7-, and 8-cut wool on monk's cloth. Designed and hooked by Jill Holmes of Northwoods Wool, Cumberland, Wisconsin, 2009.

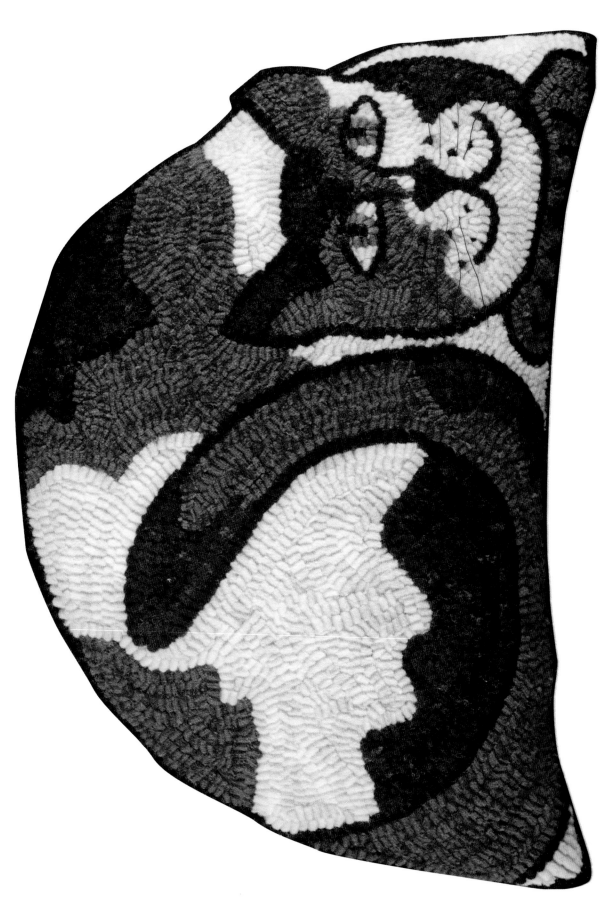

Line drawing of **Calico Cat Pillow**. Enlarge to 14" x 10" (140%).

Materials List

• 1-24" x 20" piece of monk's cloth

The following wool measurements are more than you will need to hook the cat but better that you have leftover wool than to run short.

• ¼ yard of golden/orange print
• ¼ yard of black plaid
• ¼ yard of mottled "white"
• ¼ yard of black for outline
• Scrap of green for eyes

• 1-12" x 16" piece of black wool for backing
• Black quilting thread for whiskers
• Stuffing

Jill Holmes

Jill Holmes began her love of needlework as a child mainly because of her mother, who encouraged all things creative. Once Jill learned to hook, she began to dye wool. When she had more wool than she could use, she started her own web business in 1995, www.northwoodswool. com, (715) 822-3198. Her other passion is helping teens who have behavior problems in the local high school. Jill currently resides in Cumberland, Wisconsin with her husband, Michael.

Finishing

1. The first step in finishing your pillow is to steam press it. Do this by laying your hooked piece face down and covering with a damp cloth. With your iron on a steam setting, press gently. Allow your cat to dry flat.

2. To add the whisker dots, use a strip of black yarn. Just pull up a loop here and there, dragging the yarn along the back of the face. Leave the yarn tails on the back where they will be inside the stuffed pillow. The whiskers are created using black quilting thread. Thread a needle and make a knot at the end. Pull a whisker through to the front of the cat's face. Trim it to the length that you want and repeat this process until you have enough whiskers. You can put a dab of glue on the back of your cat to hold each whisker in place if you are worried about them coming out.

3. Trim your monk's cloth to 1¹/₂" out from the hooked edge. You will need to clip the monk's cloth around the ear in order to fold the cloth back. Clip nearly to the hooking but not into it. Turn the monk's cloth back and steam press it in place. Basting it is helpful but not necessary.

4. Using a piece of tightly woven wool cut out the shape of your cat with an extra ¹/₄-¹/₂" extra all around. Holding your wool backing against the back side of your cat, begin sewing it in place. If your wool backing is

woven tightly enough, there is no need to turn under the edge. Slipstitch the backing to the edge of the monk's cloth at the very base of the loops. Use regular thread and make lots of small stitches to keep the monk's cloth from showing around the edge. Be sure to leave an opening to stuff your cat.

NOTE: *This pattern and all others shown in this book can be ordered through the* **Rug Hooking** *magazine web site at* www. rughookingmagazine.com.

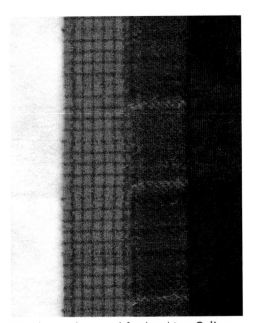

Wool samples used for hooking **Calico Cat Pillow.**

Fowl Mood

by Gene Shepherd

You've heard the question a million times. Which came first: the chicken or the egg? While chickens and eggs often show up in hooked rugs, the related philosophical question for our art form is a bit different. Which comes first—the pattern or the hand dyed wool? Although the pattern usually comes first in my process, on occasion, it's the other way around. No one was more surprised than me, after playing around with a new dye technique I was anxious to try, to suddenly be confronted with a design imperative. The wool pieces weren't even dry when I noticed that they appeared to be the perfect colors for a rooster. In this instance, the wool definitely came first and then dictated what the pattern should be.

Dyeing Transitional Wool— Without Dye

The dye method that got my creative juices going for *Fowl Mood* is a transitional wool technique that does not require any dye. It produces multi-colored pieces of wool that the fiber artist can use to soften or smooth the transition from one color to another. Diane Phillips, who learned the process from Claire de Roos and Nancy Mac Lennan, passed it to me at a rug camp. I could not wait to get home and try it since the only things needed for the process are scrap wool and a casserole pan.

While all my scraps were the same size, $^1/_{32}$ of a yard and measuring approximately $3^1/_4$" by $16^1/_2$", any odd pieces of pre-dyed wool will work equally well.

- Arrange dry pieces of wool in the bottom of a casserole pan taking care to overlap each piece at it's mid-section. For this project, thirty-two $^1/_{32}$ of a yard pieces (one yard total) were stacked in two layers. While most of the colors of wool used were not exact repeats, they did group in these color families: red (10 pieces), gold (5 pieces), yellow (5 pieces), blue (4 pieces), green (4 pieces), and purple (4 pieces).

- Mix a few drops of softening agent (Jet Dry, Synthrapol, Dawn detergent) in some tap water and carefully pour it over the dry wool. The water level should be just high enough to come to the top of the wool. There has to be enough water so that the dye, once "released" in the cooking process, can move from piece to piece, but not so high that everything mixes together.

Set the pan on top of a heat source and bring the water to a simmer. As the dry wool will soak up some of the water, a bit more may need to be added during the cooking stage. Allow the pan to "cook" until the colors start to visibly "bleed out" on each other—about 12 to 15 minutes. When it is obvious that some bleeding has occurred, the process can by stopped by adding either citric acid or vinegar. Vinegar works well in this setting as it can be poured straight from the bottle. If using citric acid crystals, dissolve a teaspoon of them in some hot water before adding to the pan.

Fowl Mood, 14" square, #8-cut wool on primitive linen, Designed and hooked by Gene Shepherd, Anaheim, California, 2009.

Cover with foil and simmer on a low heat until the dye is set again—about 20 more minutes. Rinse and dry the wool as usual.

This method produces wool that has stripes and long splotches of surprise "other" colors. The wool isn't just another pretty face—those splotches can be used in a variety of ways to make transitions from one color to another (in the way that a dip dye does) or be used to add highlights and shadows. Should an artist

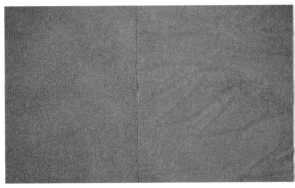

Wool samples of the dry wool achieved by the transitional dye (left) and marbleized dye (right) techniques without dye.

Line drawing used for **Fowl Mood**. Actual size is 14" square.

not want to be that particular, have no fear—beautiful wool can always be used in many different ways!

Dyeing Marbleized Wool

The two colors of solid background wool were also dyed without dye by utilizing the "marbleized" method. Dry, off the bolt, pre-dyed deep gold, light blue and light green wool were twisted, "tobacco plug" style, then simmered in a shallow pan of water with a few drops of softening agent. As with the transitional wool method, when it's obvious that colors are bleeding from one piece of wool to the next, the process can be stopped with citric acid or vinegar, before the final cooking seals the process. While I used three ¼ yard pieces of wool for this process, only the gold (⅛ yard) and blue pieces (³⁄₁₆+ yard) were used for this project.

The Pattern

Since this pattern was designed for using an #8 cut of wool, primitive bleached linen was used as the backing. The drawing shown in this article was enlarged to 13¾ " square. The easiest way to transfer a simple pattern like this is to use a light box or glass topped table. No light is even needed to transfer the basic grid that frames the design. Once that is drawn, the straight edges between paper pattern and backing can be pinned together so that the fabric cannot move. Secured in this way, even a sliding glass door, on a sunny day, will provide enough backlight to trace the rooster.

By using the transitional dye method, the resultant colors bled enough to provide good contrast for the chicken neck (wattle).

Hooking The Project

Since various reds were interspersed in the layered "bleed," some touching lighter colors and other touching darker ones, the resultant reds will come out of the casserole pan in enough different "values" to provide good contrast.

Two lighter strips (from different pieces) were used to set the comb and wattle that lies on top. Although they are from different pieces, with slightly different casts, by paying attention to the strips used, the meeting point of the two strips makes a seamless transition. The back section was hooked using strips from the darkest red.

The arc of the rooster's neck was also hooked with strips from multiple pieces. When one

Materials List

- Primitive Linen–22" x 22"

Dry wool dye method
- 3¼" x 16½" (¹/₃₂ yard) red– 10 pieces
- 3¼" x 16½" (¹/₃₂ yard) gold– 5 pieces
- 3¼" x 16½" (¹/₃₂ yard) yellow– 5 pieces
- 3¼" x 16½" (¹/₃₂ yard) blue– 4 pieces
- 3¼" x 16½" (¹/₃₂ yard) green– 4 pieces
- 3¼" x 16½" (¹/₃₂ yard) purple– 4 pieces

Marbleized wool dye method
- ¹/₈-yard yellow green
- ³/₁₆-yard blue green

piece ended, it was continued with another strip that had the same spot of color at its end. This is the first way to use these pieces. Because dye blood from more than one piece can be on any given strip, all sorts of little surprise colors start appearing in a line hooked in this fashion. It provides very interesting color twists that would not otherwise be present in most dyed wool. However, when a new piece starts with the basic color or "blush" that ended the last piece that is being continued, it creates a smooth transition, which looks like a dip dye.

While it's very tempting to play with the colored wool, one of the first things that should be hooked is the rooster's eye. One strip of black, hand cut #6 wool was used for the center iris. The eye is, in effect, a little "cat's paw" with a black center composed of hooking at 3 points around a center, unfilled, hole—the starting point will begin (and end) with the tails, while the other two points will each have a loop. The second row, hooked in a #8 cut, was made with the dullest shade of yellow/gold wool in the stash. This row should be crowded a bit as it is hooked, in order to round out the corners of the center black triangle. When hooked, a hand cut piece of #3 white was brought up in 2 holes, twisted tight, and then cut so as to leave just a spot of white highlight in the eye.

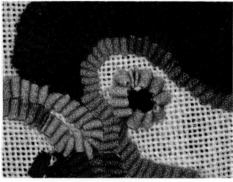

The chicken eye, hooked as a small cat's paw.

Echoing technique of hooking rows is used around the main elements and in from the border until the rows touch.

As this pattern is outlined and filled, make a point to regularly switch from piece to piece. In other words, don't hook a section with one piece until it is all used up, and then use another piece until it is all gone. Mix them as you go. Because of the transitional spots, if you want to hook a line, a darker gold that ends with a blush of red can be continued with a much lighter yellow strip—as long as it starts with a blush of red— that's the first way to use this type of wool.

Since the neck of the rooster is supposed to be feather like, this look can be achieved by hooking completely different yellows and golds next to each other. That is the second way use this wool—it takes advantage of the obvious

differences. When hooking two golds next to each other—one with a blush of green and the other with a blush of red—shadows and shading will automatically be added to that section. The wool will do the work for you as long as you pay attention to its color properties.

To make things look even more realistic, also pay attention to hook direction, turning it so the loops "finger" in to each other in wedge shaped lines. Again, in this section, notice the attempt to put different families together so their differences can be highlighted. Green golds, rosy golds, peachy yellows, and plain golds when fingered together, create a sort of striation that replicates the desired look of feathers.

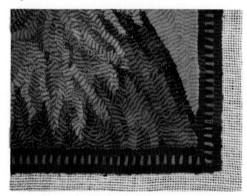

An example of fingering used to create the illusion of chicken feathers. The border is hooked with the alternate loop beading effect.

Because of all the directional and color movement present in the main characters of this design, a simple "echo" background is suggested as the best way to set off the rooster. Since marbleized blue wool with strong overtones of gold and green was used for this section, the background is any thing but flat. Yet, the rows of hooking accentuate the rooster instead of competing with it by echoing the shape of the bird. This background technique starts at the outside edges of the space to be filled and works in. In this instance, both the rooster and the outside edge of the square were outlined until those rows touched. Concentric rows are added, outside in, until the space is filled.

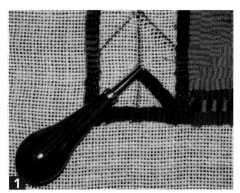

When hooking the diagonal line, keep the hook pointed at a right angle to the line being hooked. The loops will lay the direction the hook is pointing.

At the "point," change the direction of the hook so that this one loop points in a new direction. The apex of each chevron should be located in this same ditch.

After the "point," hook the downward diagonal, taking care that the hook always points at a right angle to the line being hooked. Rigidly following the same approach for each chevron will produce a very crisp geometric section.

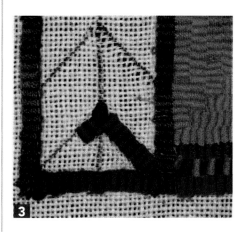

Gene Shepherd

Gene Shepherd began rug hooking in 1998. He does commission work for individuals and museums; he also designs, dyes, develops tools, teaches and writes about rug hooking His work has been featured in Rug Hooking *magazine,* ATHA Newsletter *and* Celebration of Hand-Hooked Rugs XII, XIV and XV. *Gene is the author of* The Rug Hooker's Bible *and* Prodded Hooking for Three-Dimensional Effect (Rug Hooking *magazine). He has produced two DVDs for the magazine's* Learn at Home Series *and has produced four other instructional DVDs on rug hooking for the Internet Rug Camp, a teaching blog with daily posts. Gene has been director of the Cambria Pines Rug Camp in Cambria, California since 2000. He is Senior Pastor of Anaheim First Christian Church, and lives in Anaheim with his wife, Marsha and daughter, Ann.*

Although only two very different colors of blue were used to fill in the body of the rooster, because of the color splotches that happened during the transitional dye bath, the two pieces ended up looking like 4 or 5 different related wools when cut into strips. This detail shows how dark, purplish blue strips were used to define the outside edge of the rooster. Other "blues" were tucked and fingered into the points next to the neck feathers—way #2 of how to use this wool. The reds of the alternate loop (beaded) border edge were hooked in via way #1—continuing a line with the same blush that ended it. Way #1 makes fluid lines while way #2 makes contrasting lines.

Geometric Border

The pattern is drawn with an outside border, which includes both geometric elements and words. The geometric element can easily be extended if the artist does not want a design with words. Additionally, new words can be substituted for those in the pattern.

NOTE: *This pattern and all others shown in this book can be ordered through the* **Rug Hooking** *magazine web site at www. rughookingmagazine.com.*

My Primitive Tulip

by Lois Roy/Olde Scotties Primitives

I call this rug *My Primitive Tulip.* This design was influenced by my love of antique fraktur pieces. I have always painted folk art pieces with the colors of antique frakturs. I decided that I would love to do a series of rugs featuring them. This is one of those rugs. It is a fairly simple pattern with the tulip standing out, and making the borders frame the center motif.

I fell in love with rug hooking five years ago and traded in my paintbrush for a rug hook. I find that I love the primitive antique looking rugs. The worn colors are very easy to look at. I also love to come up with new designs to use these unusual color combinations.

When I created this rug I chose to use different size strips to hook with. Doing this gives the rug an aged look. I also chose to make this rug with a dark background, but it would look wonderful with a light to medium background. If you choose to use a light background, your tulips will pop out and sing with color.

I would recommend using larger cuts and nothing smaller than a #8 cut. By doing that you would change the look of the rug. Whatever way you decide, it is a fun rug to do.

About the Wool

All of the wool in this rug is 100% wool. Choose wool with textures. This will give the rug more life and interest. I have used as is wool and some hand dyed wools. By using hand dyed wools that have a mottled effect you can achieve some wonderful shading. Another way to give your rug a primitive look is to use plaid wool. That is why I chose a dark plaid for my main color. I cut the plaid in both directions—one way for one set of strips and the reverse for another set of strips. When you hook them together you get different looks, even though they are the same wool.

The easiest way to do this is to start with one yard of wool; rip it in half, then in half again. This will give you four fat quarters of wool. Now take one fat quarter, notch and rip it at 18". When notching the wool, cut it with the selvage at the top. Then take the next 18" section cut with the selvage and rip it. Keep these separate and you will see the different colors when they are hooked. You want to make sure that all of the wools will work together.

The Cuts Used

I have used a variety of wool cuts in this rug. The cuts that were used were # 8, # 8½ and #9½. Using different cuts will give a more primitive look to your rug. It also gives your rug a softer feel.

I used #8 and #8½ in the tulip flowers and leaves. On the smaller flowers I used a #8 cut. The rest of the rug was hooked in #8½ and # 9½. Hook the borders with #9½. This gives you a great, full look; it also makes for a primitive look.

My Primitive Tulip, 34" x 20", #8-, 8½, and 9½-cut wool on linen. Designed and hooked by Lois Roy of Olde Scotties Primitives, Woonsocket, Rhode Island, 2009.

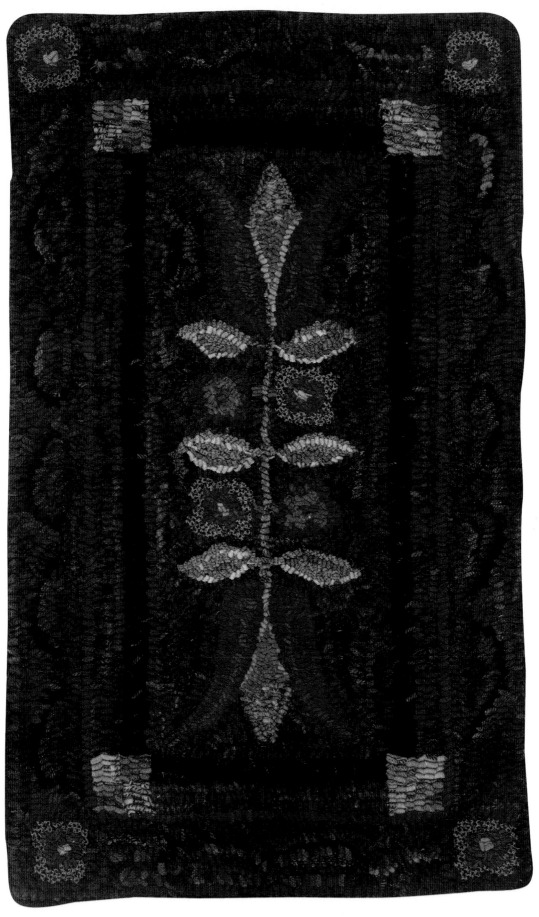

Wool samples used for hooking **My Primitive Tulip**.

Transferring the Pattern

Enlarge the pattern on a copier to the approximate size of 20" x 34". Tape the full-sized paper pattern to a light box or glass table with a light under it. Place your linen over the pattern and tape down. You should be able to see the pattern. Now take a marker and with the straight of the grain draw the main line down and then go across. This will give you the straight lines to work from. Start in the center and work out. You must keep this pattern straight or it will look out of balance. Leave 4-5" around the pattern and serge the edges. If you don't have serger, zigzag around the entire pattern.

Hooking the Rug

This rug was hooked in three sections. The middle section with the flowers and tulips was hooked first. The inside border with the checked corners was hooked next. The outer border to finish up the rug was hooked last. I found it easier to start in the center with the tulips first, then the flowers and leaves.

When hooking the rug I started with the large tulip flowers, working the center petal first, and then finishing with the outside petals. You could also hook the tulip petals all the same color and just use a darker value strip between them. I then hooked the stem between the two main tulips.

Now you are ready to hook the leaves and smaller flowers. I started with the center of the flowers using solid mustard. Hook these with #8 cut. This will allow you to have some definition in them. When hooking the leaves use a dark on the top and light on bottom. Do not outline the leaves

in all light wool. You want to have different shades in the leaf to create veining.

After you have finished hooking these parts hook a row around all that you have hooked. By doing this, it will lock in your hooked flowers and leaves. I used the main color background wool for this. Hook one row around the outside edge of the first rectangle. Now begin to hook the background around the tulips, flowers, and leaves echoing their shapes. Use different shades of darks for this part. Continue to hook until the entire background is filled in. Then hook the four corner blocks alternating colors using mustard and green with a #8½ cut.

Now hook three rows of solid black around the rectangle using #8½ cut next to three rows of the main color. Hook a row of red around the entire rectangle.

Next hook the four corners of the flowers; I hooked them all the same. Use #8 and #8½ cuts in the flowers. I hooked a row of #9½ cut around the entire outside edge and inside edge between the corners.

To hook the last four sections of the rug you can do anything you want. I have chosen a muted design in solid black #9½ cut and then filled in echoing the design in muted shades of blacks and dark wool. Continue to hook until all of the areas have been filled in.

Another idea for the outside border is to hook a hit or miss design. You can do just about anything you want. I have also made this border with a striped effect.

Line drawing used for **My Primitive Tulip**.

Lois Roy

Lois Roy is a self-taught rug hooker and folk artist, who began rug hooking seven years ago. She enjoys drawing her own designs and adapting antique rugs into patterns. Her web site, www. oldescottiesprimitives. com, (401) 765-1646, allows Lois to design and feature her rugs, patterns, hand-dyed wool, and primitives. Her rug studio, coming later this year, will be open by appointment. Lois lives in Woonsocket, Rhode Island with her husband.

Materials List

*Approximate amounts using 8, 8½, & 9½ cuts
- Reds (two matching wools)–tulip, squares, flowers & border–total fat ½ yard
- Greens (three values, light, medium, dark)–leaves & squares (3 pieces)– 3" x 18"
- Mustard (three different wools)–tulip center petal & flowers: solid mustard –3" x 18"; plaid mustard–6" x 18"; honeycomb–6" x 18"
- Solid Black–border–fat ¼ yard–18" x 28"
- Dark background main color–1 yard
- Assorted darks for background (four different wools)–fat ⅛ yard total
- Binding–matching wool piping binding
- Wool strip–3" wide x 128" long
- ¼ inch cotton cording–128" long   (3½ yards)
- Foundation linen fabric–30" x 55"

Pressing the Rug

Before finishing your rug it is a good idea to steam your piece so it will lay flat. Place a damp towel on your ironing board and lay your rug face down. Place a cotton press cloth (dampened tea towel or pillow case works well) over the rug. Press the rug with a damp press cloth with lots of steam. Press the back first, then the front. Lay rug on flat surface to dry for at least 24 hours.

Binding the Rug

You can use whatever edging you like. Whether it is cotton rug tape or yarn whipstitching, it is up to you. I would make sure if you are placing this rug on the floor you use the rug tape or whipstitch edge. Trim the excess foundation leaving at least 1¼" of foundation and serge the edge. Be sure to leave enough to work with.

Finishing with Cotton Tape

Press the backing to the back of the rug and blind stitch the finishing tape right next to the last row of hooking, then blind-stitch the opposite side of the tape to the back of the rug.

Whipstitch the Edge

Choose a piece of cording that matches the height of your loops and is long enough to go around the rug plus 2" longer. Turn the excess foundation to the back, encasing the cording so that the cording lies snugly against the last hooked row. Using a heavy-duty thread place a running stitch to anchor the cording. Where the two pieces meet, butt them together. Whip stitch with quality worsted weight yarn. Now you can use cotton-binding tape to cover the excess foundation on the back of the rug.

I used a binding with a piping effect. Cut strips of cotton cording and a dark wool 3" wide and 128" long. Stitch the cording into a pocket of wool. Then stitch the binding as close to the hooked edge as you can. Fold over to the back of the rug. Be sure to miter the corners and stitch the back down. I like this method, but I don't put my rugs on the floor.

Labeling

After you finish your rug, please take the time to make a label for it. It is essential to include your name and date; you could also include the name of your rug and designer of the rug. If your rug was made for a special event or person, include that information. You can make your own label or purchase a label. There are many different ways you can sign and date your rug. I have used a piece of old ticking that I printed my information on. I think that tends to add to the antique look of the rug. You also might want to hook your initials and date in the border of the rug. Whatever you decide to do, please date and sign the rug.

NOTE: *This pattern and all others shown in this book can be ordered through the* Rug Hooking *magazine web site at* www. rughookingmagazine.com.

Peaceful Garden, Hooked Door Pocket

by Sharon Soule/Crow Hill Primitives

This is a great project for using up all those wool scraps you have on hand. I used a #12 cut strip so this project worked up quickly. Don't let a #12 cut intimidate you. If you do decide to hook this in a wide cut, it helps immensely to use a wide shank hook such as a Hartman. This project can just as easily be hooked in smaller cuts.

Enlarge and transfer the pattern onto your backing using the method you prefer. Sew on binding tape or coordinating 1¼" wool strip along the drawn line as you would for a rug and zigzag stitch ¼" outside of binding. Using the background wool, hook a row or two as close to the binding as possible. This will help keep the linen backing from showing through when you sew the bag together and hold the shape of the bag as it is hooked.

Hooking

Hook the outlines of the motifs first making sure you stay on the inside of the lines so the motifs won't grow too large. Then hook a row of background around them to help hold the shape. Go back and fill in all the motifs. I started hooking the body outline of the dove first and then her wing, followed by the flowers and mushrooms. If you are wondering what the pink lump is on the bottom right, it's one of many healing stones that I always plant in my own gardens. After the motifs are hooked and the background is done, check the back of the project for holidays and fix them if needed. Then steam the piece on a thick towel right side down. Trim the linen close to the stitching and press in the corners of the backing diagonally followed by the four sides and let it sit until dry.

Putting the Bag Together

Next, take the piece of wool you are using for the back, fold the top edge back (wrong sides together) and baste using a contrasting thread color. Place this on top of your hooked piece wrong sides together. Making sure the top edges are even, pin or baste top edges together. This will prevent the top edges from slipping while the bag is being put together. Fold in the remaining sides and bottom to match the hooked piece. I find it easier to do this with the piece lying flat on a table rather than in my lap. Then, using contrasting thread, baste a large X from corner to corner through the front and back. This may seem like a lot of basting but it helps the piece stays nice and flat and won't shift while you are stitching it together. Use matching upholstery thread to stitch your front and back together. I used a ladder stitch for this. Remember to leave the top unstitched! After you are finished stitching it all together, you can go ahead and remove the basted X.

Lining

Take your coordinating cotton fabric and cut two pieces 12½" x 14". Stitch the sides and bottom of the lining fabric together (right sides together) using a ¼" seam. Turn top edge down ¾" and finger press. Insert lining into

Peaceful Garden, 12" x 13", #12-cut wool on linen. Designed and hooked by Sharon Soule of Crow Hill Primitives, Kennebunkport, Maine, 2009.

Sample of how handle was made—alternative for a braided handle

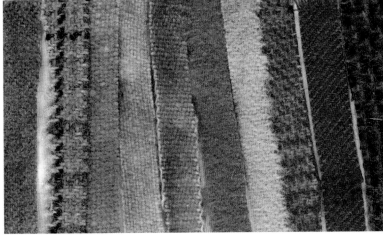

Blue flower | Flower centers and beak | Flowers

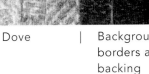

Rose|Mushrooms|Bleeding | Leaves, ground and worms | Dove | Background | Background
quartz   hearts   borders and
crystal   backing

hooked bag. If you plan on using this project as a door pocket, you may want to sandwich a sturdy piece of cardboard, slightly smaller than the bag, between the lining and back before stitching it closed. After the lining is stitched down remove basting stitches around the top edge of the bag.

Strap

I put my selvage strips to good use by making braided handles for my bags. For this bag I used three different coordinating colors and left the raw edges showing to give a more primitive look. If your selvage strips are too short, sew a couple of strips together end to end to make your strip long enough for braiding. The length of your braid depends on how long you want your strap to be. My braid measures 28" from knot to knot. To make the strap, start by tying the three strips into an overhand knot leaving approximately a 4" tail. Braid the three strips together and end it in another knot and a 4" tail. To attach the handle, stitch the knots to the outside top of your bag at the side seams about 1" down using upholstery

Line drawing used for **Peaceful Garden**. Enlarge to 12" x 13".

thread for strength. On the inside of the bag stitch on the buttons to cover the knots left from stitching the handle on.

This was made to hang on my mudroom door and hold a bouquet of flowers. You can even use real flowers if you insert a gallon size zip lock bag inside the pocket to hold water. This project could also easily be made into a pillow by adding stuffing or a pillow form and stitching all four sides closed. You could also use it as an over-the-shoulder bag.

NOTE: *This pattern and all others shown in this book can be ordered through the* Rug Hooking *magazine web site at* www. rughookingmagazine.com.

Materials List

- The sample piece measures 12" x 13". Remember that wool amounts are approximate and were measured after the wools were washed and dried. The actual wool amounts needed depend on the individual wool, the cut used and your own personal hooking style.
- Pattern–16" x 17" linen
- Dirt–5" x 16" piece of greenish brown wool
- Background–3-5 dark brown wools totaling 28" x 16" Cut strips of each, mix them up and hook in randomly, or you could also put all of your background wools in a dye pot and dye them together, marrying the colors.
- Dove–2-4 oatmeal wools totaling 14" x 16"
- Stems, leaves, and worms–3-5 green wools totaling 7" x 16"
- Mushrooms–2-3 wools totaling 3" x 16" light gray

- Rose quartz–1" x 16" light pink
- Flowers–2 pink wools totaling 3" x 16"
- Flowers–2-3 blue wools totaling 5" x 16"
- Beak, flower center, flowers–4-5 gold wools totaling 7" x 16"
- 1½ yard binding tape or 1¼" wide wool strip to match background wool (I used the wool strip).
- Back of bag–15" x 15" piece of dark brown wool
- Bag lining–½ yard cotton fabric
- Hardboard or cardboard (optional) cut slightly smaller than your finished bag
- Basting thread in contrasting color
- Upholstery thread in matching color
- Needle
- Thimble
- Pins
- Scissors
- 2 large buttons

Sharon Soule

Sharon has been hooking since the mid 1970s. Her husband had been doing carpentry work at Joan Moshimer's rug hooking studio and saw Joan's work and thought it would be something his wife would be interested in. He surprised her with a kit and everything she would need to try out the new craft. She started hooking with a fine cut but soon discovered that the primitive style is what really made her heart sing. She has been hooking primitive ever since. Sharon and her daughter, Alicia, have been offering their own patterns and hand dyed wool since 2000 under the name of Crow Hill Primitives, www. crowhillprimitives.com, (207) 967-0573.

Sheep Sampler

by Wendy Barton-Miller/The Red Saltbox

My love of old samplers and the occasional reproduction samplers I have designed and stitched were my inspiration for designing *Sheep Sampler*. Taking my love of stitching those old alphabets, and combining it with my love of wool and sheep, made *Sheep Sampler* the perfect project for me to happily hook up just for fun!

Transferring the Pattern

Enlarge pattern on a copier to the size of 11" x 25". Tape the full size paper pattern down onto a light box or table, or use a glass coffee or dining table with a lamp underneath. I like to use light/bleached primitive linen so I can easily see through the rug backing to the pattern underneath. Place your linen on top of your paper pattern template and draw the outer border lines of the pattern with your permanent marker, making sure to draw your straight lines on the grain of your linen. Once you've drawn the outer rectangle and straight lines of your rug, draw the inner elements of the pattern onto your linen. The letters of the alphabet are not drawn straight; they are staggered up and down for a nice folksy effect. Serge or zigzag the edges of your linen to prevent fraying during the hooking process. Or you can use masking tape if a sewing machine is not accessible to you.

Let's Hook

The *Sheep Sampler* rug was hooked in #8 cut wool strips. *Note for beginners: Remember to always hook inside the lines of the motifs of your rug. You may hook right on the straight lines for your border lines and for the letters.*

First, hook your sheep head and legs in the darker valued wool and then hook your sheep's body in the grungy oatmeal wool. Remember when hooking to outline the area first with one row of hooking and then hook inside that row to fill in the subject in your rug. As soon as I finish hooking a motif like the sheep in this rug, I like to immediately hook one row of my background wool around that motif. That will "lock" the shape of the motif and keep it crisp as I move around and hook other elements of the rug. Hook one row of your tan plaid background wool around the sheep motif.

Now hook the stars in the mustard wool. I used an over dyed plaid wool for my mustard stars. Remember to hook one row of mustard to outline each star and to hook inside the lines. Then hook inside the stars to fill them.

Move on to the letters of the alphabet. You will hook on the lines of the letters and then hook one row of background wool around each letter to lock its shape and keep your letters crisp.

Using the dark value textured wool, hook the outer rectangle shape of the rug with one row of hooking. Also hook the border line above the bottom hit or miss section in the dark value wool.

Sheep Sampler, 11" x 25", #8-cut wool on Scottish primitive linen. Designed and hooked by Wendy Barton-Miller, Attica, Indiana, 2009.

Line drawing for **Sheep Sampler**.

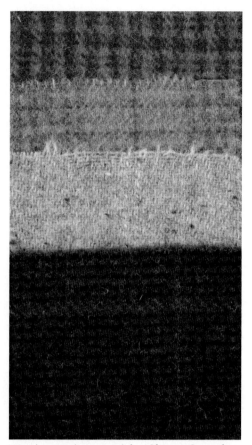

Wool swatches used for **Sheep Sampler**.

Tip from Wendy

If you are intimidated when hooking letters and numbers, try this: don't think of them as letters and numbers. I tell my beginners to think of letters and numbers simply as lines. Hook them as you would any flower stem or borderline. Do not get caught up in your hooking not resembling a particular letter. Hook them as lines and outline them with one row of your background wool and move onto the next. When you are done hooking all of your "lines", you will be able to stand back and see that you have actually hooked letters!

Hook the background of your rug with the medium value tan plaid wool. A busy background will overpower a rug like this and you will lose your alphabet as one of the main motifs of the rug. So keep your background wool selection on the calm side and be sure it's a muted plaid or texture. I like to use the echo technique when hooking a busy design like this sampler rug. The echo technique for a background is when you outline a motif with one row of hooking of the background wool, then continue to fill in the background by hooking rows around that motif, over and over, until the background is completely filled. With this rug, I hooked around each of the letters echoing its shape, until it joined with the echoed rows of the letter or motif next to it.

Hook the hit or miss sections of your rug last, once you have established the colors of the

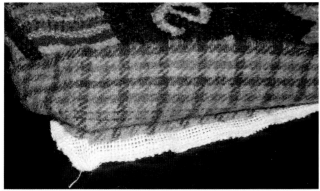

1. Binding with wool strip example. The wool strip is sewn up close to last row of hooking with nylon carpet thread.

2. The wool strip folded and pinned down to backside (enclosing raw rug backing edge), as you would if using rug tape. Miter corner nicely and pin in place.

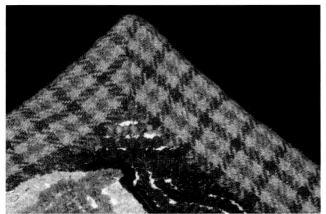

3. The wool strip is hemmed down to back of rug using nylon carpet thread. Hem the mitered corners down neatly.

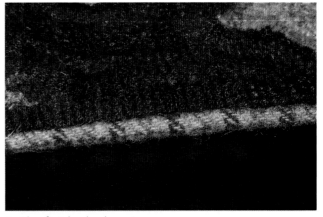

4. The finished edge view.

Draw word or name first, this dictates overall width of your custom rug. Note that letters are staggered up and down for a folksy effect and are spaced approximately 1" apart.

motifs in your rug. I like to use a bit of the colors of wool I used in the motifs of my rugs, in the hit or miss sections to compliment the main motifs. In *Sheep Sampler*, I made sure to use the mustard of my stars at least once in the two top diagonal corner hit or miss sections, and then repeated mustard several times in the bottom rectangle hit or miss section. I also wanted some red and robin's egg blue in my rug, so I evenly scattered some red and robins egg blue strips throughout my hit or miss sections. That sprinkles the dominant red and robin's egg blue colors evenly over the rug, even though there was no red or robin's egg blue in any motif of my rug. Many of the other wools used in the hit or miss are not dominant colors, just various neutrals of grungy tans, browns, grays, etc. Hook in whatever color wool strips you have available in your leftover stash of strips. Use fewer grungy neutrals and add more colors to the hit or miss, for a more vibrant color result. *Sheep Sampler* is a rug that is bland in color, until you hook the hit or miss sections. The hit or miss sections dictate the colors of this rug, since the motifs are not varied shades of color.

Finishing Your Rug

Press your rug with lots of steam, using a cotton towel between your iron and your finished rug. Press the back of your rug, and then turn it over and press the front of your rug. Repeat if necessary. Remember to use lots of steam. If your rug has lost its rectangular shape during the hooking process, now is the time to tug your rug into a nice rectangle again. Lay the rug on a flat surface and let it dry overnight.

Bind the rug with the technique of your

choice. This rug was bound using a 2" wide strip of wool (dark value texture) instead of rug tape. If your strip of wool is not long enough to go completely around your rug, sew 2" wool strips together to form the proper length to go all the way around your rug. The excess rug foundation was serged off (or cut off and zigzagged with a sewing machine). The 2" strip of wool was sewn on just as you would sew on rug tape. It was sewn very closely to the last row of hooking with a carpet/nylon thread. Then it was folded over to the back of the rug, and hemmed down, making sure to miter and sew the corners of the wool/rug tape down neatly. Refer to binding photos for various steps of this binding technique, photos #5, #6, #7, #8. Now give your rug another quick steam pressing to crisp up the edges of your rug. Set aside and let it dry flat overnight.

Optional Beads

If you would like your sheep to have eyes, you can sew tiny glass beads at this time. Using the carpet/nylon thread, sew glass beads onto the top of the pile of loops of your rug. I chose to leave my sheep plain with no eyes, which gives a more simple finished result.

Fun Variation for this Rug Design

This rug is a great one to personalize with your family name, a special date in your life, or even with your favorite quote. Common words you could use: simplify, welcome, faith, love, friends, etc. You could also personalize it using rug hooking words such as wool or rug hooker. Trace whatever word or name you want, using the letters from your pattern template as the pattern for each of the letters. If the word or name you chose is longer, your hooked rug will become whatever width is necessary to accommodate your word. Draw your word or name onto your blank rug backing first, since that will dictate how wide your finished rug will be. For an example, refer to photo #4. I chose to hook my last name, so I used the appropriate letters from the pattern template to form my last

Wendy Barton-Miller

Variation of **Sheep Sampler** using letters to form personalized family name rug, 11" x 16", #8½-cut wool on Scottish primitive linen. Designed and hooked by Wendy Barton-Miller, Attica, Indiana, 2009. Various wools of similar colors were used to hook the stars and the background for a scrappy finished result.

Wendy Barton-Miller first picked up a rug hook in 1999, and today is the primitive rug designer and teacher behind The Red Saltbox. Known for her use of textured wool and primitive color palette in wide cuts, her low contrast rugs have an instant old age appearance. She is an award winning rug artist, author of the primitive dye book Recipes From The Kitchen of The Red Saltbox, *a frequent contributor to* Rug Hooking *magazine and a member of ATHA. More information about Wendy and her rugs can be found online at www. theredsaltbox.com.*

name. Leave approximately one inch between each of your letters and all around your word or name. I staggered my letters up and down just slightly, to give the finished rug a real folksy finished result. Draw one letter slightly up, the next slightly down, then the next letter up again slightly, and repeat for entire word. Draw your hit or miss bottom section below your chosen word or name (approximately 1" below). Center your star and sheep motifs above your word or name (approximately 1" above your word or name), and add the diagonal hit or miss sections in the top corners to balance your overall design. If your name or word is especially long, you can add more stars across above.

For a fun hooking variation and effect, note that I used many different mustard wools in my stars for this example. Go through your left over wool strips, sorting out only mustards to use. Now hook those mustards into the rug for your stars randomly for a great primitive result. The background is also a combination of many different dark valued wools, dark value wool strips that were sorted out of my left over wool strip bin.

NOTE: *This pattern and all others shown in this book can be ordered through the* **Rug Hooking** *magazine web site at* www. rughookingmagazine.com.

Sheep's in the Meadow Footstool

by Connie Litfin and Marti Taylor/Mustard Seed Primitive Designs

We all remember the nursery rhyme "Little Boy Blue" from our childhood. You may not take your naps under a haystack, but you can put your feet up on your hooked footstool and relax. Whether you use our design as a footstool or a tablemat we hope you will enjoy hooking it. We have given you two border options for completing your rug. Choose whichever you prefer. Wool requirements and directions are given for both rugs.

Transferring the Pattern

The finished size of *Sheep's in the Meadow* is 11" x 16", which is the also the measurement of the footstool (available through Mustard Seed Primitive Designs. For ordering information, see Resources, page 88.) We have used monk's cloth as our backing material but burlap or linen would also be appropriate backing.

Cut your backing material 19" x 24". This allows the extra 4" on all sides for ease in hooking when the design is in the frame. To prevent raveling, serge or zigzag the edges. (*Hooker's Hint:* If you do not have access to a sewing machine, use masking tape along the edges.)

To find the center of your backing, fold it in quarters and mark the center with a pencil. Using a ruler at the center mark measure 5½" above and below the center and 8" out from side to side. Then measure 2½" in on each side. To draw the lines, drag a pencil point along the holes. This will ensure that the lines are straight along the grain of the backing. Trace the lines with a permanent marker.

The pattern provided in the book will need to be enlarged at 200%. The easiest way is to take the pattern to a copy center and have it enlarged. Our favorite method of transferring the pattern to the backing is to trace the design onto Red Dot Tracer (available from Mustard Seed Primitive Designs). Center the design inside the marked lines of your canvas and pin in place. Trace your design with a permanent marker. Red Dot Tracer is porous and will allow the marker to bleed through to the backing. Remove the Red Dot Tracer and go over any light areas again with your marker. You can either free hand your circles or purchase a template with different size circles at an office supply store. (*Hooker's Hint:* Trace the design on the Red Dot Tracer with a ballpoint pen. That way when using the permanent marker you will be able to see if you have all areas traced onto the canvas.)

Sheep's in the Meadow (footstool), 11" x 16", #6- and 8-cut wool on monk's cloth. Designed and hooked by Connie Litfin and Marti Taylor of Mustard Seed Primitives, Indianapolis, Indiana, 2009.

Choosing Your Wool

We will identify the different projects by identifying them as footstool or mat. Behind the sheep on both projects we choose to do a hit or miss background using various shades and textures of green.

Footstool: Dark green/black textured wool was used for the rug outline and the background of the tongues. The sheep was hooked with a small tan check and black for the face and legs. Use a dull green/blue for the eye. To keep the subtle look, the sheep curls are a few shades darker than the check. The center of the penny circles is dark green, with a medium green and gold on the outside ring. The tongues are a red check.

Mat: A small green/black check was used for the rug outline and the background of the penny circles. Your sheep can be any color you choose. A small gray check was used for the sheep and black for the face and legs. The sheep curls are a darker gray, which makes them subtle and not a focal point. Any color wool can be used for the penny circles. We chose gold for the center, then blue and red. You can choose to hook them all the same as we did or mix them up with different

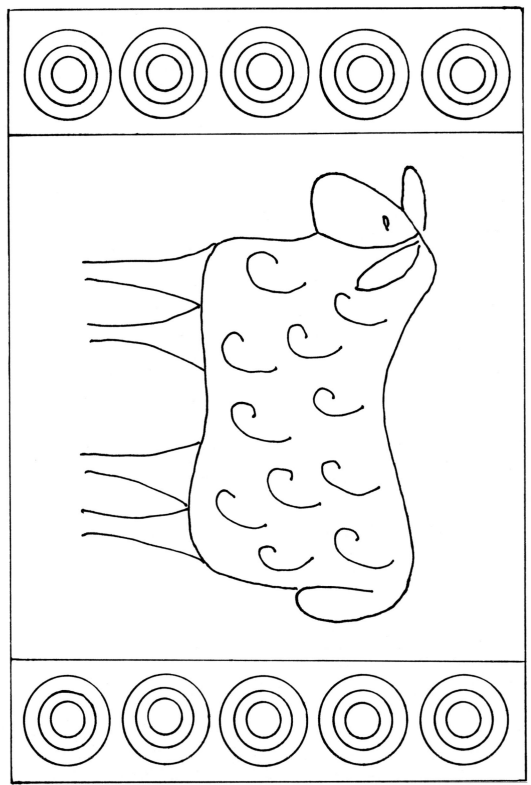

Line drawing used for **Sheep's in the Meadow.**

colored wools. (*Hooker's Hint:* Don't be afraid to use textured wools. Textured wools are plaids, checks, herringbones and heathers. They give your project a more primitive look and will reflect the look seen in an old rug and add interest and movement to your rug.)

Cutting Your Wool

Refer to the supplies list before cutting your wool. Both #6 and #8 cuts were used in the project. (*Hooker's Hint:* Make sure your wool is cut on the straight of grain. To keep it straight, tear your wool along the straight of the grain parallel to the selvage. Use pieces 6-8" wide. While stripping, it may be necessary to tear the wool piece again to keep the grain straight.)

Hooking the Design

Footstool: Begin by hooking the outline of the sheep's body. Hook one loop for the eye. Outline and fill in the face and legs. Hook the curls on the sheep's body and fill in the sheep. Next, hook around the outer edge of the rug. This will stabilize the rug and make it easier to hook the background. The background was hooked in straight lines in alternating directions. Follow the design lines on the pattern. Once the background is completed, hook the penny circles. Start in the center and work your way out. Outline the tongues and fill in. To fill in the background, hook a row of the green/black around the tongues. Continue filling in the background until all areas are filled.

   Mat: Begin by hooking the outline of the sheep's body. Outline and fill in the face and legs. Hook the curls on the sheep's body and fill in the sheep. Next, hook around the outer edge of the rug and the line separating the sheep and penny circles. This will stabilize the rug and make it easier to hook the background. The background was hooked in straight, horizontal lines. Once the background is completed, hook the penny circles. Start in the center of the circle and work your way out. To fill in the background, hook a row of the green/black check around each penny circle. Continue filling in the background until all areas are filled. (**Hooker's Hint:** Always hook just inside the pattern lines to avoid distortion. If you hook on the line or outside the lines you will need more wool, as your design will be larger.)

Finishing the Rug

Many methods can be used to finish a rug. Each rug hooker has his or her favorite technique. You may like to try different ways to see which you prefer.

   Both Projects: When the hooking is finished, stitch approximately ½" from the last row. Trim the backing to 1" and serge or zigzag around the edge, cutting off the corner points. Lay the rug flat with the backside up on a hard,

Materials List		
Both Projects		**Mat**

Both Projects
- 19" x 24" Canvas
- Red Dot Tracer
- Fine point permanent marker

Footstool
- 6" x 16" black for face/legs (#6 cut)
- 10" x 16" tan check for sheep body
- 2" x 16" darker tan for sheep curls (#6 cut)
- 18" x 16" green/black for outline of rug and background of tongues
- 45" x 16" assorted greens for sheep background (mix well when hooking)
- 2" x 16" dark green for center of penny circles
- 3" x 16" medium green for middle of penny circles
- 4" x 16" gold for outer edge of penny circles
- 12" x 16" red check for tongues
- 1 strip dull green/blue for eye (#6 cut)

Mat
- 6" x 16" black for face/legs (#6 cut)
- 10" x 16" gray for sheep body
- 2" x 16" darker gray for sheep curls (#6 cut)
- 18" x 16" green/black for outline of rug and background of pennies
- 45" x 16" assorted greens for sheep background (mix well when hooking)
- 4" x 16" gold for center of penny circles
- 3" x 16" blue for middle of penny circles
- 4" x 16" red for outer edge of penny circles
- 1 2/3 yards binding tape

Wool yarn
* All wool is #8 cut unless indicated otherwise.

flat surface. Fold the edge of the backing even with the last row of hooking and miter the corners. Place a wet towel over the rug, and using a hot iron, steam the entire surface of the rug. Steam the edges and corners flat. Flip the rug over making sure the edges of the backing are laying flat. Steam the front of the rug as you did the back. Lay rug flat to dry for approximately 24 hours. (**Hooker's Hint:** Don't scoot the iron over the surface of the rug. This may distort the shape of the rug. Pick the iron up and move it. Steaming also improves the look of your loops and evens their height.)

   Footstool: We used a slightly different finishing method that would allow us to either attach with Velcro (so we could change designs) or tack the rug down permanently. We didn't want the footstool to be totally flat, so we used

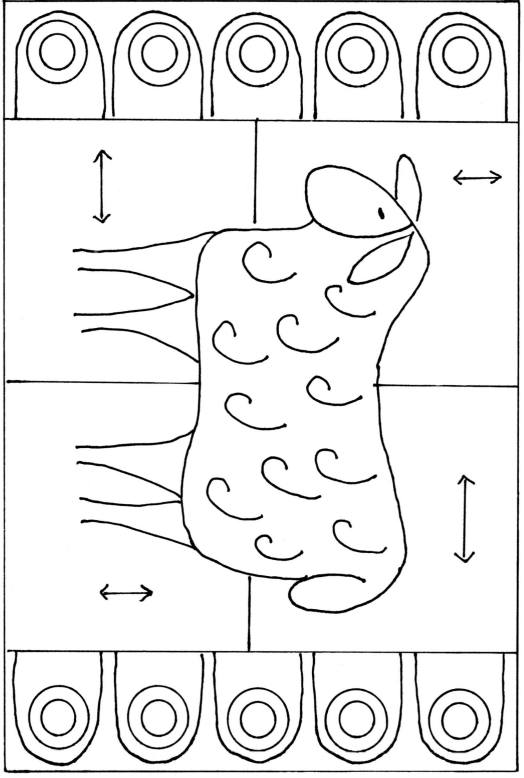

quilt batting under the rug. You will need to cut two pieces of batting. Cut one 9" x 14" and one 10" x 15". Flip the rug over to the back and layer the batting with the larger piece on top. Tack the batting in place with needle and thread to prevent shifting. Finish the back by cutting a piece of wool 12½" x 17½". Center the wool on the back of the rug, turn under the edges and whipstitch the wool piece to the rug going between loops on the last row of hooking. Sew as close to the edge as you can to prevent any of the canvas from showing. You can now attach the rug

Sheep's in the Meadow (mat), 11" x 16", #6- and 8-cut wool on monk's cloth. Designed by and hooked by Connie Litfin and Marti Taylor of Mustard Seed Primitives, Indianapolis, Indiana, 2009.

Marti Taylor

Connie Litfin

Connie Litfin and Marti Taylor are owners of Mustard Seed Primitive Designs. For a color catalog of their designs, send $5 to Mustard Seed Primitive Designs, 5528 W. 62nd Street, Indianapolis, IN 46268. Their online store is available at www. mustardseedprimitive designs.com.

to the footstool by using Velcro or small nails.

Mat: We finished the mat by using rug binding tape and 3-ply wool yarn. We attached the binding tape as we whipped the edge with the yarn. To begin, separate the yarn so it is not twisted and thread three strands in a blunt darning needle. Do not start in a corner. Lay your binding tape along the edge of the last row of hooking, insert your needle underneath the folded backing edge and pull yarn up at the last row of hooking. Bringing the needle and yarn toward you, catch the binding tape about ¼" down and pull yarn through. Continue around the rug mitering the corners. You will need to insert the needle in every hole of the backing so that you cannot see the backing peeking through. Once this is finished, whip stitch the binding tape in place. Now, curl up in your favorite chair, prop up your feet and relax!

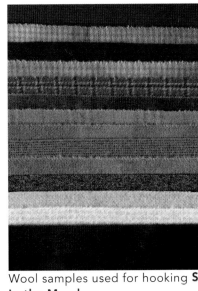

Wool samples used for hooking **Sheep's in the Meadow**.

NOTE: *This pattern and all others shown in this book can be ordered through the* **Rug Hooking** *magazine web site at* www. rughookingmagazine. com.

Sherman

by Jeanne Field with Lois Reesor/Rittermere-Hurst-Field

The idea for the *Sherman* rug was first conceived as a wedding rug for friends who have a boxer named, of course, Sherman. It was designed and hooked by Lois Reesor with help from a few friends. Our idea was to do a large rug for beside the bed. Although it is not a busy rug, we feel the beauty of the rug is in its simplicity. Looking at several antique rugs influenced the scroll design. They have a timeless appeal that carries them through from the past to the present. We also played with the shape of the oval to fit the image of the dog so it would not look too big or too small within the oval. We used a silhouette of a boxer and then colored it to match the real dog, a brindled boxer. The single line of the border brings the rust color to the outside of the rug.

We purposefully left more room on the bottom side of the oval for lettering. In the case of *Sherman*, we used WordArt on the computer to form the letters in a font we liked and then stretched them to make them look dog-bone shaped.

Every rug is a learning experience. Lois had never hooked scrolls, so I pencil-shaded a drawing and she dyed three textures and plain wool inspired by the colors in a transitional swatch. Since the scrolls were not done in fine shading, they fit in well with the primitive style of the rug. She found it an easy and effective way to hook scrolls.

The antique black background was chosen because we like dark backgrounds and it would make the scrolls stand out. It also took the color of the outside edge of the rug into the center as the dog was a similar color. The light beige behind the dog gives the rug a brightness to contrast with the antique black background and highlights the boxer. The rust was chosen as it complimented the antique black and the beige and looked good as a vein in the scrolls.

You may want to order the pattern with the oval blank to put your own design inside. Another dog, cat, or horse can be used, or be creative and put in a scene from your memories. If you decide to apply your own image to the center of the rug take heed of our experience. We were waiting for a picture of the dog to come, but wanted to get started hooking so started with the scrolls and the background. By the time we had the image of the dog sorted, the oval's border was finished as well. We ended up with the inside of the oval unhooked and very puckered. This made it difficult to apply the dog to the linen-and we had to be careful of how we hooked it (looser than normal to ease in the excess linen backing) to cut down on the bumps when finished. It also took a good pressing at the dry cleaners to flatten this section of the rug. Get to know your local dry cleaner and stress that no water is to be used—only steam to press rugs to prevent colors running. We have had a couple of instances of people taking their rugs to the dry cleaner for pressing and not stressing no water is to be used and a couple of the colors ran—so sad.

Sherman, 45½" x 28", #7-cut wool on primitive linen. Designed by Rittermere-Hurst-Field. Hooked by Lois Reesor, Aurora, Ontario, 2009. A true primitive hooked on linen.

Line drawing used for **Sherman.**

With the roll, pin, and whip method of finishing, there is no need for either cording or binding. The rolled backing acts as the cording and the outside edge is turned in so there is no need for binding. It is a quick and effective way to finish a rug—the *Sherman* rug was whipped in five hours.

Order of Hooking

My suggestion is that you start in the center and work your way out to the border.

1. Hook the dog with color E and the lines under his feet with color D (See wool samples on p. 59). The patches on the chest and feet are done with Dorr natural. (Not shown.)

2. Hook behind the dog with light beige (color C). Hook one row around the dog and the lines under his feet and one row around the inner oval line. Hook the rest of this area in curvy lines. See diagram.

3. Hook oval, dogs' name, and line next to border in color B.

4. Hook the scrolls. Begin with the rust texture (color B) for the vein. Hook the blue/green (color F) next to the vein and another row beside it. Bring in the dark green, then the medium working toward the ends of the scrolls. Finish the tips with the lightest green. See diagram.

5. Now to hook the background behind the scrolls. Hook one row of color A around each scroll and the line next to the border. This area should be filled in as you did it around the dog, in curvy lines.

Finishing

1. Roll, Pin and Whip Method

2. With sewing machine using zigzag stitch or stay stitching, sew 1" from your hooked outline. To create less bulk during whipping, as you approach the corners sew on a diagonal ¾" out from the tip of the hooking. You are reducing the amount of burlap you need to roll for whipping. Cut excess burlap from the finished piece outside the stay-stitch line.

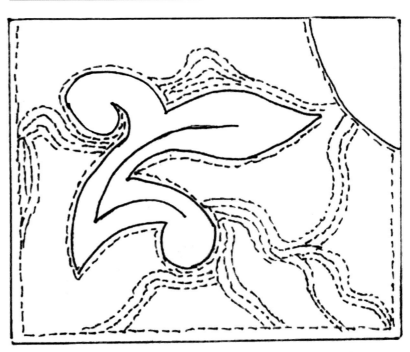

Filling in background with curvy lines makes the background quiet so that the motifs stand out.

Materials List

Wool Amounts:

- Main background (behind scrolls)–1½ yards
- Rust border (oval and border line)–½ yard rust texture as is. The rust was also used in the veins of the scrolls.
- Background behind Sherman–¾ yard
- Sherman's Shadow–1/32 yard
- Sherman–¼ yard
- Scrolls-Blue Green–¼ yard
- Dark Green–⅛ yard
- Medium Green–⅛ yard
- Light Green–1/16 yard
- Sherman's white patches–1/16 yard Dorr natural (not shown in photo)

Before putting your hook to the design, take time and do this—if part of your design is shaded, use the simple trick of pencil shading to help you. First you need to make two copies of your design on an 8½" x 11" piece of paper. On one, pencil shade from dark to light. On the other, using pastels or colored pencils shade from dark to light. This will give you a three dimensional effect in black and white and one in color. These will guide you in the shading of your motif. Give it a try.

Pencil shading helps in placing the wool in the correct order to give a three-dimensional effect on the scrolls. It gives you actual colors to relate to as you hook.

3. It is now time to press your piece for the first time. Place a thick bath towel on your ironing board with your hooked piece wrong side up and put a dampened tea towel on top of your hooking. Press your work by moving the iron from place to place, holding it in place for a few seconds. Do not run your iron in a back and forth motion. When one side is done turn your work over and do the same thing on the right side of your piece.

4. With right side of work facing you, roll the burlap tightly in towards the hooked edge, pin, and baste. At the corners, mitre and roll to the front keeping a rounded corner (not squared). You will need to roll tightly and work the corner area.

5. Using 100% wool, 2-ply yarn (2 yards at a time) thread on to a tapestry needle or large blunt darning needle. You will whip with a double thickness of yarn.

6. Start whipping in the middle of one side, have the right side of hooking facing you. Secure yarn and work from the front to the back keeping close to the last row of hooking.

7. Whip the folded edge by taking the yarn from the front over the rolled burlap edge to the back. Insert the needle into the next hole as you comeback to the front. Pull the yarn tightly as you whip but not so tight as to buckle your edge. Keep repeating this making sure that no backing shows and it is neat. *Note: Whipping must butt up against the last row of hooking.

8. Press the rug once more and your piece is finished.

Dye Formulas

*CBW stands for cup of boiling water.
1. Main Background-behind scrolls-Antique Black over ½ yard Claret cashmere and wool
   - 1¼ tsp Majic Carpet black in 1½ CBW
   - ¾ tsp Majic Carpet bottle green in 1½ CBW
   - 2 tbsp white vinegar or 1 tbsp citric acid in each dye solution.

Soak wool then squeeze out excess water and scrunch in a 9" x 13" pan. Put each dye solution on in spots until all used. Wearing rubber gloves push down on wool to distribute dye. Bake at 200 degrees F for 1 hour until water is clear. Rinse and hang to dye.

2. *Sherman* - Antique Black over ½ yard of medium brown. Same Formula and method as above.

| A | B | C | D | E | F | G | H | I |

Wool samples used for hooking **Sherman**.

Jeanne Field

3. Background behind Sherman–Over ½-yard natural wool
   - $^1/_{64}$ Majic Carpet Blue
   - $^1/_{64}$ Majic Carpet Seal Brown mixed in 1 CBW.
   - Open pan dye, use vinegar or citric acid to set. The same formula was used for the shadow below the dog-over ¼-yard natural.

4. Scrolls - Four colors were used in the scrolls, dyed over different wools:
   Blue/Green–main body–over ¼-yard Dorr Glen Plaid
   - $^1/_8$ tsp Majic Carpet Blue
   - $^1/_8$ tsp Majic Carpet Bottle Green
   - $^1/_{32}$ tsp Majic Carpet Black

   Mix all dyes in 1 CBW and open pan dye. Set with vinegar or citric acid.

a) Dark Green-over ¼-yard Dorr Glen Plaid
   - $^3/_{32}$ tsp Majic Carpet Brilliant Green
   - $^1/_{32}$ tsp Majic Carpet Bottle Green
   - $^1/_{32}$ tsp Majic Carpet Chocolate Brown

Mix all dyes in 1 CBW and open pan dye. Set with vinegar or citric acid.

b) Medium Green-over ¼-yard Oatmeal
   - $^1/_{32}$ tsp Majic Carpet Moss Green
   - $^1/_{32}$ tsp Majic Carpet Bottle Green

Mix all dyes in 1 CBW and open pan dye. Set with vinegar or citric acid.

c) Light Green-over ¼-yard Dorr natural
   - $^1/_{64}$ tsp Majic Carpet Moss Green
   - $^1/_{64}$ tsp Majic Carpet Bottle Green

Mix all dyes in 1 CBW and open pan dye. Set with vinegar or citric acid.

Jeanne Field is the senior partner in Rittermere-Hurst-Field. She has been hooking and teaching for over 45 years and is a contributing editor to Rug Hooking *magazine. Lois Reesor started working for Jeanne ten years ago and has taken on many jobs such as printing, dyeing, and going to hook-ins and shows. She has been hooking for ten years making rugs for weddings, nieces and nephews. She made a 50" x 36" story rug for her parents' 50th anniversary. Someday she will make one for herself.*

NOTE: *This pattern and all others shown in this book can be ordered through the* Rug Hooking *magazine web site at* www.rughookingmagazine.com.

Snow Day

by Shelley Flannery and Barbara A. Hanson/Threads of Comfort Designs

Warm blue with a touch of sunny yellow, *Snow Day* celebrates the first hint of spring as winter withdraws with a smile. *Snow Day* is one of a series of stories from Threads of Comfort Designs revolving around the imaginary citizens inhabiting the village of Bunsea.

Tips for This Rug—Letting the Wool do the Work

We search high and low for bolt wool in plaids, textures, and multi-colors that serve as a workhorse for the coloring and texture in our designs.

The hat in *Snow Day* is a textured honeycomb from Rebecca Erb of The Wool Studio. A true chameleon, this wool looks like sunflower seeds when hooked into the middle of petals, works as slithery snakeskin, and is a great bubbly texture for our snowman's hat.

Our snowman's scarf is a fuchsia/orange/violet plaid from Heavens to Betsy (see p. 88). Hooking in straight rows across the color ways in this plaid provides a jumble of color that simulates a knit scarf when worked in rows. Fussy cutting of the same material can provide different values, and colors that are married prove to be very useful in your rug—think flowers or a rooster's tail.

Nancy Miller Quigley's marvelous dark layered custom dye makes for merging shadows in our trees using one wool piece for multiple shades and depth.

And, that mistake in the dye pot? We did not intend our lightest value khaki to have rust over dyed, but our "oops" moment in the dye kitchen gave us just the right touch in context of the other khakis and deep greens used in *Snow Day's* trees.

Pattern Preparation

Enlarge the pattern 200% to 12" x 12" using gridded paper or your local photocopy service. Prepare a 20" x 20" fabric backing by sewing or serging the outside edges to prevent fraying. Trace the pattern onto the backing with a permanent fabric marker proven to be colorfast and non-bleeding, leaving a 4" margin around the outside of the pattern.

We use a light table to transfer designs to the backing; a sufficiently large window surface with good back lighting makes a good substitute.

Hooking the Design

Outline the outside edges of the design using the sky, snowman, scarf, and tree color as appropriate. Next outline all elements in the design.

Snowman's Hat: Hook two rows of yellow for the hatband before filling in the hat with the honeycomb textured wool. We hooked the hat in horizontal lines parallel to the hatband. Putting this wool through the washer and dryer felted the texture, pulling a looser weave nicely together.

Snowman: First hook the eyes and nose with #6 cut black and the snowman's mouth with #4 cut black raising the loops slightly higher than the background. We hook the circles of eyes and nose from the outside in, placing one loop in the center of every circle. Finding fewer loops gives the most impact.

Snow Day (hooked rug), 12" x 12", #4-, 6-, and 8-cut wool on monk's cloth. Designed and hooked by Shelley Flannery and Barbara A. Hanson of Threads of Comfort Designs, Hillsboro, Oregon, 2009.

Buttons: Hook the buttons in similar fashion, again, raising the loops higher than you would the background, allowing the #6 cut to hold its own against the larger #8 cut of the background.

Background: Fill in the background of the snowman's body and face with creamy textured wool. We found our choice of Rebecca Erb's blond plaid on natural to give the warmth we prefer over a starker white. We worked a figure either pattern around the buttons in the snowman's body, hooking them from the inside to the outer edges of his figure.

Scarf: The knot on the scarf is hooked in circular rows. The two tails are hooked in straight lines to the bottom edge of the design

Line drawing used for **Snow Day**.

to simulate knitting. Cutting across the full length of the Heavens to Betsy plaid gave us a happy jumble of colors married to one another that pick up other colors in the trees and hat.

Sky: We kept the hooking simple for the sky, echoing the outlines of the snowman and trees. An abrash dye of Emma Lou's Sky Blue gives the sky depth with the warm blue shifting softly from light to medium and back again.

Trees: Five shades of green are used for the trees in *Snow Day*. We selected yellow-toned greens as opposed to cooler blue-toned, compatible with the warm-toned neutral used in the snowman's body.

Throwing a variety of wools together for depth and shading is one of our favorite activities. Try tossing all five colors suggested for the trees in *Snow Day* into a heap, blindly pull a strip from the heap and hook. We confess that we snuck a few of the darker greens and black to outline a tree's branches but left the rest to land serendipitously.

Both trees are hooked in lines beginning at the center of the tree extending outward to the tips of the branches. Notice that the tree in the

Wool samples used for hooking **Snow Day**.

Materials List

- Backing–20" x 20" backing of choice. We used monk's cloth this time, but often select primitive linen for our designs.
- Marker–Rub-a-Dub permanent fabric marker or other felt pen to be proven to be colorfast and non-bleeding. Be warned! Felt marker bleeding to the surface of your rug is a sad event.
- Finishing material–9" x 18" piece of wool for binding edges.
- Wool–all #8 cut with exception of #4 cut for the mouth and #6 cut for eyes, nose, and buttons. Measurements refer to pieces of 100% wool used throughout.
- Sky–12" x 18" warm blue
- Hat and buttons–6" x 18" textured black
- Snowman face and body–15" x 18" warm neutral
- Eyes, nose, and mouth–3" x 18" black
- Scarf–9" x 18" plaid
- Trees–five 3" x 18" strips of varied greens

foreground is slightly lighter and brighter than the one behind the snowman.

Options: Try sewing antique buttons on for the snowman's body or needle felting them with wool roving and felting needle. We love combining the textures of buttons and other fibers with the hooked loops of wool.

Finishing

Before steaming, trim all hooked ends, shaping eyes, nose, and buttons by cutting away any background wool desired.

We use a double folded towel for cushioning on the ironing board or flat vinyl surface, placing the hooked piece face down on the towel. Wet a second

Snow Day, (penny rug), 12" x 12", various wool cut for wool appliqué of the background, snowman's hat, snowman, scarf, and evergreen trees. Designed and hooked by Shelley Flannery and Barbara A. Hanson of Threads of Comfort Designs, Hillsboro, Oregon, 2009.

Penny Wool Instructions

- Duplicate the pattern pieces on freezer paper. Cut out shapes from the freezer paper.
- Iron freezer paper shapes to wool. Cut out wool shapes around the freezer paper, and then peel the freezer paper off.
- Place the evergreen tree on the background in the top upper left hand corner. You may anchor with tacky glue.
- Place second evergreen tree to the right on the background.
- Now, place snowman's body on the background with the evergreen trees tucked under the snowman's body.
- Place scarf on top of snowman's neck and body.
- Next place scarf ends as shown.
- Place knot to complete scarf.
- Place hat on the snowman's head.
- Next place the hatband on top of the hat, anchoring with tacky glue.
- Center eyes and nose and anchor with tacky glue.
- Blanket stitch around all the edges of pieces using DMC Perle cotton, size 5.
- Option—Use wool roving with a felting needle to needle-felt the eyes, hat band, and other details as desired.
- Use an outline stitch for the snowman's mouth. Add three old buttons or needle felt them to complete your project.

towel, wring it out, and place it over the hooked piece in a single layer. Press down without moving the iron for 15-20 second then move to another section and repeat. When the back is finished, flip the hooked piece over and repeat the steaming process, rewetting and wringing out the covering towel as needed. When top is done, find a place to lay your rug to dry. Don't move it for 24 hours.

Finishing the Edges

Bind or whip the edges in the finishing method you prefer. We like using wool from the hooking, making a 2" wide strip to use as rug tape. Cut the backing to within 1¼" of the finished edge, folding it toward the back after serging, or sewing, the edge to prevent fraying.

Sew a folded edge of the 2" wide wool to the front, catching the edges of the last row of hooking. Once this is done, fold the wool to the back and whip a folded edge to the back of the rug, mitering the wool strip at the four corners, completing the edging.

NOTE: *This pattern and all others shown in this book can be ordered through the* **Rug Hooking** *magazine web site at* **www. rughookingmagazine.com.**

Shelley Flannery

Barbara A. Hanson.

Life-long friends and sisters in spirit, Shelley Flannery and Barbara A. Hanson are the duo comprising Threads of Comfort designs. They also co-own Rug Art and Supply in Hillsboro, Oregon. Shelley and husband, Mark, have three children – Harrison, Ben, and Olivia. Barbara and husband, Dale, share their home with daughters Jessica, Chloe, and Abby and the physical storefront of Rug Art and Supply. Both live in Hillsboro, Oregon. Avid quilters for more than two decades each, the two took a rug hooking class together and never looked back. Now, designing, teaching, rug hooking, attending retreats and helping support Las Rancheritas—the rug hooking project of Agustin Gonzales, Mexico, keep them happily busy in an art form they love.

Tulip Basket Runner

by Karen Worthington/The Blue Tulip

This pattern was hooked with my dining room table and the colors in that room in mind. Pick colors of your choice, but pay attention to make sure that there is enough contrast between the basket, flowers, and background. If I don't like my color combinations after I've started hooking them, I pull them out and try again. Don't be afraid of choosing different colors than the ones I've chosen. The gold wools in this pattern were actually my last choice for this rug. Then, after I decided on the different values, I added the gold to the flowers (they were tan first). Three of the gold wools used were the same dye formula, just different wools used in the dye pot.

Transferring the Pattern

Outline your paper pattern with a black Sharpie to make tracing the pattern easier. If you used bleached primitive linen, as I did, simply lay the pattern on a table and place your linen on top. You will be able to see your pattern underneath and easily be able to transfer the design. Otherwise, you can use Red Dot Tracer or a light box to transfer your design. Outline the borders of your pattern first, making sure you stay straight in the grain of your backing material.

Hooking the Pattern

This entire rug was hooked in #8-cut wool using off-the-bolt textured wools as well as dyed wool.

I started hooking the basket in the center first. Hook the red diamond in the middle first outlining it and then fill it in to the middle.

Hook the two red triangles next and then hook the rest of the basket in the tan. Next, hook the stems of the flowers with the lighter color green wool and then outline the leaves in the same wool. Fill in the leaves with the darker green wool. Hook the flowers using the lightest color gold for the two center areas of the flower and then hook the red outer area of the flower.

Once you've finished hooking the center basket and flowers you can start hooking in the background wool. Outline the entire basket, flowers and leaves and the border of the diamond first and then fill in. I used two different wools for the darker black/brown background of each tulip basket. They are both off-the-bolt wools and look great together. Simply use them interchangeably as you hook; pick up one strip of one color and then the other and so forth.

Hook the gold wools next, starting with the lightest value, first hooking three rows. Take the next value of gold and hook three lines again. When you get to the next value of gold hook two lines and then the diamond. Hook the diamond in red and tan and then add another line of the third value of gold. The darkest value of gold wool is hooked next (3 rows) followed by the brown textured wool (3 rows again), followed by the last piece of the background wool, which is the dark brown wool. Continue hooking the rest of the design as indicated. There is one hooked line of red around the entire border and then two hooked lines of the solid brown background wool.

Tulip Basket Runner, 36" x 13", #8-cut wool on primitive linen. Designed and hooked by Karen Worthington, The Blue Tulip, Harmony, New Jersey, 2009.

Line drawing used for
Tulip Basket Runner.

NOTE: *This pattern
and all others shown in
this book can be ordered
through the* Rug Hooking
magazine web site at www.
rughookingmagazine.
com.

Wool samples used for **Tulip Basket Runner**.

Materials List

Approximate amounts
- 44" x 21" piece of bleached primitive linen serge or zigzag stitch along edges
- $3/8$ yard of textured black/brown wool
- $1/2$ yard of brown wool
- $1/4$ + $2/16$ yard of brightest gold wool
- $1/4$-yard medium gold wool
- $1/16$-yard medium dark gold wool
- $1/16$-yard dark gold wool
- $1/16$-yard brown textured wool
- $1/16$-yard tan wool
- $1/16$-yard dark green textured wool
- $1/16$-yard dyed medium green wool
- $1/4$-yard dark red textured wool
- 30 yards brown whipping yarn
- 3 yards cording

Karen Worthington

Karen Worthington inherited her love of primitive antiques and hand-made things from her parents and their friends. She enjoyed quilting and needlepoint before learning how to hook rugs. Karen prefers her rugs to look old so she uses mostly muted colors and primitive designs. She has a studio in her home where she designs her rugs, dyes wool, and teaches rug hooking. Karen lives with her husband Bill, two daughters, Rebecca and Gretchen, their dogs, Heidi and Ozzie, and one Maine Coon cat, Cami. For more information about Karen, visit her web site at www. thebluetulipwoolery.com, (908) 859-6350.

Finishing

Once you've completed all of the hooking, give this rug a quick steam. At this point it is narrow and does tend to curl a bit, especially if you hook as tightly as I do. This will make whipping the edges a little easier for you. If your rug is not curling, you can skip this step and just steam the whole rug when you are finished whipping the edges.

Lay a thick towel on a safe surface and place your rug face down on top of it. Place a damp towel on top of your rug and with your iron on its highest setting; steam the edges of your rug, rewetting the top towel as necessary. The entire rug will be steamed again when you finish whipping the edges. Let your rug dry before whipping the edges.

Cut your linen about 1" to 1½" away from your hooking, rounding the corners, and zigzag or serge the edges. With your rug upside down, lay the cording on the linen and roll towards your hooking. Pin in place. Using a jumbo

bent tapestry needle, thread with yarn and start whipping, leaving a 1" tail that you will whip over to cover. Work back to front, getting close to your hooked area making sure to pull tight on the yarn and cover all of the linen. When whipping the corners, you will have to use more yarn in order to cover all of the linen. When you get close to the end of your yarn in the needle, weave the last 1" back through the whipped yarn on the back of the rug and then cut.

Press/steam your rug again, paying special attention to the whipped edges that will curl the most. Steam the back and then the front. Let dry flat for 24 hours.

Complete kits can be purchased from The Blue Tulip at *www.thebluetulipwoolery.com*. Kits include design hand-drawn on primitive linen, uncut wool, directions, color picture and whipping yarn. Cost is $175 plus $10 shipping.

Under The Willow

by Kris Miller/Spruce Ridge Studios

This adorable wall hanging was inspired by my young Wensleydale sheep, Emma, who has been seen chasing birds across her pasture.

Hooking the Wool Strips

1. Trace your pattern onto a 30" x 34" piece of backing with a permanent marker. These measurements allow at least an extra 4" margin around all sides of your pattern. I hooked my wall hanging on primitive linen.

2. Start by hooking the tree trunk and branches with the brown plaid. For added interest and variation, I randomly hooked a few strips of contrast texture into the trunk of the tree. The branches are hooked as a single row.

3. Before you begin to hook the leaves, count the number of leaves on each branch and mentally divide them into three groups. The first group will be the leaves closest to the tree trunk. You will want to hook these with the wool that has the darkest green value. Some of the smaller branches may only have one or two leaves that are this color. The second group will be the leaves that are growing in the middle portion of the branches. These should be hooked with the medium value of green. The longest branch will have a few more middle leaves and the shortest branches will have a few less. The third group of leaves will be those that are toward the ends of the branches. Use the lightest green value for these, including the leaf that is on the very tip of the branch. Again, the longest branch will have more and the shortest branches will have less.

4. Hook the wings of the bird with antique paisley. Carefully cut your paisley in the same direction as the long threads that are woven on the back. Use a #8½ cut, or at least one size larger than the rest of the wool strips you are using. Trim any loose threads that come to the surface of your work with scissors.

5. You may wish to hook the eye of the bird first before you begin filling in its body. I started with a small strip of antique black wool for the center of the eye. I pulled up an end, hooked one loop, and then pulled up the other end. I continued with a narrow strip of dull yellow texture, hooking a circle around the center of the eye. Outline and fill in the entire body of the bird with the red herringbone. Don't worry about putting in the feathers on the bird's head right now; they will be hooked in later.

6. Using the antique black wool, hook the lamb's ears and facial features. Fill in the lamb's face with the light gray/taupe texture. You will notice that the lamb's body will not be filled in with the roving at this point. It is better to do this hooking at the very end of your project for several reasons. First, as you hook with roving, it will fluff out and fill in your hooking area. For this reason, it is much easier to pull roving up against hooked wool strips. Secondly, it is best to minimize the exposure of the wool roving against the

Under the Willow, 22" x 25", #8½-, 8-, and 6-cut wool on linen. Designed and hooked by Kris Miller of Spruce Ridge Studios, Howell, Michigan, 2009.

gripper strips of your rug hooking frame. These strips can tear and pull at the roving. Extra care and caution is needed when stretching a roving/hooked area over your frame. If you are using a rug hooking frame with an open hooking area of at least 10" x 13½", you should be able to center the area of the lamb's body on your frame and the roving can be hooked entirely without moving your work. Lastly, you do not want to expose the hooked roving to heat and steam because it will flatten the roving

Line drawing used for **Under the Willow**.

and may even felt it or cause it to shrink. Therefore, for the best and most desirable results, the roving should be hooked in after your rug has had its finishing pressed with your steam iron.

7. Begin filling in the background. I used a mixture of a light golden brown plaid, a dull maize check, and a brighter maize texture and hooked them randomly. Hook one row of background around all of the objects, including the empty space for the lamb's body. When hooking around the spot for the lamb's body, make sure that you are hooking just outside the drawn line to accommodate

*Hooked entirely with textured wool in #8½, #8, and #6 cut strips, wool roving, sheep's locks, and eyelash yarn.

*All wool measurements are approximate. Your results may vary depending on how high or low you hook.

- 30" x 34" piece of linen or monk's cloth.
- A primitive rug hook.
- A rug hooking frame (not a hoop).
- ½ yard golden plaid for border, cut in #8½
- 7/8 yard light golden brown plaid for background, cut in #8½
- 5/8 yard maize check for background, cut in #8½
- 6" x 14" brighter maize texture (optional) for highlights in background, cut in #8½
- 21" x 16" brown plaid for tree trunk, cut in #8½
- A few strips of contrast texture for highlights in tree trunk, cut in #8½
- Three values of green/yellow texture for leaves, all cut in #8½
- 8" x 17" darker value for leaves closest to the tree trunk
- 9" x 16" medium value for middle leaves
- 10" x 15" lighter value for lower leaves

- 14" x 17" olive green/orange windowpane plaid for ground, cut in #8½.
- 5" x 14" red herringbone for bird's body, cut in #8.
- A small piece of antique paisley, approximately 2" x 20", for bird's wing, cut in #8½
- 1 strip of dull yellow texture for bird's eye cut in #6.
- 3" x 16" antique black for the sheep's ears (cut in #8½). Used also for the sheep's eyes and mouth and the bird's eye (cut in #6).
- 4" x 16" light gray/taupe texture for sheep's face, cut in #8.
- 1½-2 ounces of Corriedale roving for sheep's body. Roving is available for purchase through Spruce Ridge Studios.
- 4-6 pieces of curly sheep's locks (eyelash yarn or other novelty/textured yarn may also be used) for accent around sheep's face. Sheep's locks are available for purchase through Spruce Ridge Studios.
- 1 yard of eyelash yarn (hooked as a double strand) for feathers on bird's head.
- 35-40 yards of worsted weight yarn for whipping the rug's edges.
- 3 yards of twill tape for hemming rug.

the roving. Continue filling in the background, echoing around all the shapes to give a nice soft movement to the entire piece. If you are also using the optional brighter maize texture in your background, use it sparingly to highlight random spots around the rug. For example, I used it in a few small areas around the bird, the lamb's head, and around the tips of a few leaves. It will give hints of a "glow," but you don't want these areas to "pop out" too much. Remember that "less is more" in this situation.

8. As you are filling in the background, hook the ground area with the olive green/orange

Wool samples used for hooking **Under the Willow.**

wool. Remember to hook just outside the drawn line of the lamb to accommodate the roving.

9. Hook the border with the golden plaid, making sure you hook two straight rows around the entire outside edge.

10. After you have completed hooking all the fabric strips, thoroughly steam your rug with a steam iron and a damp cotton press cloth, back and front, set it aside, and let it dry flat for at least 24 hours.

Hooking with Roving

Roving is the clean, combed wool from a fiber-bearing animal. It looks like a long fluffy "rope" that is an inch or two in diameter. I chose wool roving that came from the fleece of a Corriedale sheep. It has a creamy off-white color and a wonderful texture that is easy to hook. To prepare your roving for hooking, you must do several preliminary steps:

- Grasp the long "rope" of roving in your hands and pull off a piece about 18" in length. The ends will be wispy. Start at one wispy end and gently pull the roving apart lengthwise to separate it into two pieces.

- Grasp one of the half-pieces of roving in both hands with your hands about 6" apart. Pull slowly and gently with your hands so that you can feel the fibers begin to separate but do not pull apart the roving. Your goal is to gently open up and loosen the roving so that it will be a little fluffier and easier to hook. Reposition your hands farther down the roving and repeat. The piece should be approximately $^3/_4$" in diameter. The size of your hooked loops will depend on the diameter of your roving strip.

- Hook the roving just like you would hook a wide-cut fabric strip. You must always use a primitive hook so you are less likely to split the fibers when pulling up the loops. Always bring your ends to the top of your work and trim them evenly. When you end your roving strip, begin a new piece in the same hole, just as you would do for a fabric strip.

- Each time you pull up a loop of roving, roll your hook toward the previous loop. This will keep you from pulling out the previous loop.
- Space your loops at least 2-3 threads apart. Don't pack your loops. Don't worry if your loops are not perfectly even. A sheep's fleece is not perfectly even either.

Begin by hooking an outline row of roving around the entire space for the lamb's body. For best results, make sure you pull the roving loops up a little higher than the wool strips. This gives a nice dimension to the lamb. Hook one row of roving around the lamb's face and then continue to follow the shape of the body until the entire space is filled.

Once the roving is entirely hooked in, you can add a few sheep's locks or curls to the top of the lamb's head. Pull up these curls in between the roving and the wool strips hooked for the face. You will hook them similarly to a wool strip. Pull up one end of the sheep's curls so that the end hangs out about ³/₄"-1" high. Now hook a loop with the sheep's curls, but pull it up so it forms a large high loop (do not pull out the end). Continue in this manner until you get to the end of the curl, then pull up the other end so that it hangs out about ³/₄"-1". Continue with another sheep curl, pulling up the end in the same opening where the previous curl ended. You may also use an eyelash yarn or other textured novelty yarn instead of sheep's curls.

To embellish the bird's head with "feathers," use a double strand of coordinating eyelash yarn. Hook it in the same way as the sheep's curls by "wedging" the yarn in between the loops of the bird's head and the background. Pull the eyelash yarn up very high with your hook to release the "eyelashes" and then pull the yarn back down so that it is just slightly higher than the hooked loops. Bring the ends of the yarn to the top of your work and trim them to about ½" so that they are even with the "eyelashes."

Take your mat to your sewing machine and sew small, straight stitches around the entire piece approximately ¼" from the finished hooked edge, taking care not to catch the toe of your presser foot in the outermost row of loops. Use a zigzag stitch and sew on top of the row of straight stitching that you just sewed. Repeat this process ¼" from the first row of stitching. Use a worsted weight yarn that matches your border color and thread the yarn through a bent tip tapestry needle. Work from the back of your hooking. I fold my linen over a scant ¼". Holding the twill tape next to the edge, I whip the wool yarn around the folded edge of the linen. I catch a small portion of the twill tape while I am whipping, thus finishing the edge and attaching the tape at the same time. After I have finished whipping with the yarn, I trim away the excess linen to within 1" of my hooking and hand sew the other edge of the twill tape to the rug with a slipstitch.

NOTE: *This pattern and all others shown in this book can be ordered through the* Rug Hooking *magazine web site at* www. rughookingmagazine.com.

Kris Miller

Kris Miller is a self-taught rug hooker who specializes in primitive designs with textured wool and wide cuts. She is the owner of Spruce Ridge Studios, selling primitive rug hooking patterns, hand-dyed and as-is wool, a wide variety of rug hooking supplies, and roving. Items may be purchased by mail order or by appointment to visit her studio. Kris has won many awards and ribbons for her rugs, including two honorable mentions in A Celebration Of Hand-Hooked Rugs XIII *and* XVI. *Her original designs have also been featured as pattern inserts in* Rug Hooking *magazine and the book* Projects For Primitive Rug Hookers. *She has taught at many workshops and rug camps across the United States. Kris lives in Howell, Michigan with her husband, two sons, and an assortment of Angora goats, sheep, cats, and dogs. For further information contact Kris Miller, Spruce Ridge Studios, www. spruceridgestudios.com, 517-546-7732.*

Very Veggie Runner

by Martha Reeder and Liz Quebe/GoingGray

Need a perfect reminder to get your three to five vegetable servings per day? Hook this fun table runner as your dietary guide, spring planting inspiration, or teaching tool for your favorite toddler. Who knew vegetables could be so versatile? New vegetable hybrids are always cropping up so be bold with your color selections—even carrots are purple nowadays.

Pattern Preparation

This pattern measures 12" x 27". Place your pattern on a light box or on a glass table with a light underneath to illuminate the work surface. Center the pattern underneath your backing of choice. Draw the outside edge of your pattern first. Come in 4" to 5" from the cut edge and, using a Sharpie, *carefully* follow the grain of the backing or the 'ditch.' Take care to get your pattern on the backing straight. Now draw the veggies and don't forget to check that all of them are on the backing before you put the light away. It's easy to miss those roots!

Size of Cut

Though *Very Veggie* can be hooked using a fine cut, I prefer a wider cut and hooked most of my piece using #7. The details, such as the lines and roots in the onion and garlic, were hooked with a #5 cut. I often use multiple cuts to achieve the effects I want in my hooked pieces. When you do this, it is important to keep the narrower cut high to match the height of the larger cut used. You can easily lose a narrower strip as it recedes into the rug.

Hooking the Wools

Begin with the eggplant (who can resist purple wool?). Starting just inside the lines, hook the eggplant by contour hooking along the outline and filling in directionally lengthwise along the vegetable. Place and anchor the highlight early. Use a medium-value green texture to complete the stem.

Now, just like a garden pest, move on to the tomatoes. Hook the stems first, using the same green texture that you used in the eggplant. Using a red of your choice, outline the tomato and then fill it in directionally from top to bottom. Repeat this for the smaller tomato with another red. If you end up with fabrics too close in value, you can put a narrow dark line just along the top edge of the small tomato where it meets the larger one.

Using the green-yellow texture designated for the carrot tops, cut a few narrow strips and hook the horizontal lines in the carrots. Outline the carrots with your orange wool and hook the lengths of the carrots until they are complete. Take a few strips of the darker gray-green value and hook a few loops where the green tops intersect the carrot body; also put some loops where any shadows might be. This will give the tops some depth and interest.

The onion will require some narrow-cut strips to mimic onionskin. Put in the roots, and take a bit of your background color and anchor the roots by hooking a bit of background around

---

Very Veggie, 12" x 27", #5, #7-, and 8-cut wool on monk's cloth. Designed by Liz Quebe and hooked by Martha Reeder of GoingGray, Rochester, Minnesota, 2009.

Line drawing used for **Very Veggie.**

them. Continue to put in the onionskin lines, but don't outline all of the outside edges, as it will not look natural. Fill the rest of the onion with your orange-rust selection. Sometimes selected wool values are too close, and you may need a darker value to 'pop' the subject. This happened to me with my border and I opted to add some darker rust value to bring out the onion.

The greens of the scallions mix light, medium, and dark values. Place the dark green furthest away and work your way forward using the medium and light values. It's fun to give the impression of some dirt on the bulb. Make the roots dirty with your gray texture.

Skip over to the garlic and hook it in the same manner as the onion, substituting the garlic colors. I opted to put in some purple, as it's always nice to carry your colors around the rug.

The incorporation of the peas and peapods into the border adds a distinctive element to this pattern. To address any value problems, I opted to make the outside of the peapods dark. Hook these using the other dark green wool and use another medium green for the other outside pod. Use a medium green for the peas in the pods and complete the inside pods with two different light greens. Finish your peas (where have we heard that before?), which are scattered on the borderline, with a variety of your greens, taking care to keep your colors and values balanced.

As you work on your rug, continually put in some background. After 'setting' a row of background around a veggie, continue filling in, keeping your hooking curvaceous to make it interesting. Complete your hooking with the border.

- Backing Materials of Choice—22" x 36" monk's cloth, linen, or rug warp (Allows for a generous 5" around pattern)

Wools

Note: wool amounts are estimates, assuming a #7-8 cut and #5 cut for details

Item	Area	Size	Wool
Eggplant	Body	8" x 16"	Deep purple marbleized or spot dye
	Highlight	1" x 16"	Medium value purple* Also used in garlic lines
	Stem	7" x 17"	Medium green overdyed texture* Also used in scallions and tomato stems
Large Tomato	Body	8" x 17"	Overdyed red plaid or other suitable tomato color
Small Tomato	Body	2" x 17"	Lighter value red plaid or tomato color of choise
	Stems		Medium green overdyed texture* Also used in scallions and eggplant stem
Carrots	Body	7" x 17"	Orange plaid or other carrot color of choice
	Green Tops	6" x 17"	Green-yellow texture
		1" x 17"	Dark gray-green texture
Round Onion	Body	3" x 18"	Orange-rust marbleized or spot dye
	Lines	1" x 17"	Rust-brown
Garlic	Body	3" x 16"	Natural with teeny texture* Also used in scallions
	Body	1" x 16"	Lavender over dyed texture
	Roots	1" x 17"	Medium gray texture* Also used in scallion roots
Scallions	Body-White		Natural with teeny texture* Also used in garlic
	Body-Green	4" x 17"	Light green spot dye* Also used in Peapods and Peas
			Medium green overdyed texture* Also used in eggplant and tomato stems
		2" x 17"	Dark marbleized or spot dye* Also used in peas
Peapods	Both	2" x 17"	Hunter green
		2" x 17"	Medium green herringbone
		2" x 17"	Light green
Peas			Use various greens from all vegetables
Background		3/8 yd	Peach cream herringbone
Border		1/8 + yd	Beige/peach windowpane

Indicates fabric used in other vegetables. Reference the photograph.

Finishing—Cording–2 1/2 yards (optional)
Yarn for whipping edge
Rug Binding–2 1/2 yards

Finishing

Before you begin any finishing work, steam your piece so it will lay flat. Place a towel on your ironing board and put the rug face down on the towel. Dampen a cotton press cloth (a tea towel will do just fine) and steam the piece. Don't slide the iron around; simply lift the iron up and down, moving around the piece using light pressure.

Wool samples used for hooking the **Very Veggie** design.

Martha Reeder

Liz Quebe

GoingGray is the business of third-generation rug hooker Martha Reeder, who has a studio in Rochester, MN. She is aided and abetted by her artist sister, Liz Quebe, who comes up with pattern designs. The name is a reference to their maiden name and the natural state of their hair color. GoingGray patterns are inspired by the good things in everyday life, and overlaid with whimsy. For more information about GoingGray and all of its offerings, visit the website at www.GoingGray.com or make an appointment to visit Martha at her studio. Contact her for your rug hooking needs through the website or at (507) 285-9414.

Technique: Marbleizing wool

This fun technique, developed by Karen Kahle of Primitive Spirit Rugs, is an easy way to create your own wool colors without investing in any dye products. Picture a wool sandwich. Place a piece of light-colored wool between two pieces of medium and dark values and complementary colors—that's the sandwich. Now roll it into a log, tie it with twine, and twist it up. (Just like us, the more wrinkles, the more character.) Place the roll in a cook pot. Add a tablespoon or two of laundry detergent and a tablespoon of a wetting agent, such as Jet Dry. Fill the pot with water until the wool is two-thirds wet and simmer for 20-30 minutes. This is where the magic happens, as the wools 'bleed' into adjacent layers. Take a peek and if you are satisfied, set your colors by adding 1 teaspoon of citric acid or ½ cup vinegar. Simmer 15 minutes more, then rinse and dry. Don't hesitate to experiment with this no-dye technique. If you don't like what you get, throw it back on the stove in another combination. It's always a surprise.

I used three marbleized wools in *Very Veggie*. For the eggplant, I used a light blue and two varying purples, and used one of the darker purples to hook the body. The onion incorporates marbleized wool from a rust/camel/orange combination. A few peas are hooked using marbleized green wool.

Repeat this procedure on the right side of the rug, and then let it sit for 24 hours until it is totally dry.

Using a small zigzag stitch, sew around the perimeter of the hooked area. Sew a second line of zigzag stitches 1¼" out from the first, and then cut off the excess backing outside of the second line of stitching. If you have a serger, it will nicely cut and finish this edge. Placing a radius at the corners helps eliminate excess fabric.

Finishing is an integral part of a hooked rug; it can make or break your piece. Rug hooking literature illustrates many methods of finishing. I favor the use of cording and whipping the edge, as I believe it is the most durable and professional finish. Turn the excess foundation to the back, encasing the cording so that it lies snugly against the last hooked row. With a heavy-duty thread, baste the cording around the rug using running stitch. Butt the two ends of the cording where they intersect. Whip the edge with a quality worsted-weight yarn. Follow this with the application of the rug binding to cover the foundation edge. Using an overcast stitch, secure it to the backing (not the loops). *Hint:* It helps to do this on a flat surface. Repeat this technique for the second edge, mitering the corners to keep them flat. Now you've finally found a way to enjoy your veggies. Mom would be proud.

NOTE: *This pattern and all others shown in this book can be ordered through the* Rug Hooking *magazine web site at www. rughookingmagazine.com.*

Wooly Saltbox Cozy

A Teresa Kogut Design by Kim Kowula/Prim N Proper Stitches

I've been meaning to hook this design for some time now and have always envisioned it to be a cozy. And, what a cozy it turned out to be! I made this cozy large enough to cover my cutter and wood base, but you can easily adjust the size to fit a tea pot or simply hook it as a hot pad. On the back of another hooked version of this cozy, I transferred the sheep along the bottom edge and wrote "My Wooly Home" in the center. If you saw my house, no truer words have ever been spoken! You can also use up those extra strips with a hit or miss on the back. I hope you will enjoy hooking this project as much as I did.

Instructions

1. Start by enlarging the pattern by 300% to 12$\frac{1}{2}$" x 17".
2. Copy outline to red dot tracer with a Sharpie
3. Serge, zigzag, or tape monk's cloth to stop fraying
4. Using the bottom for your straight of grain, center Red Dot pattern piece on monk's cloth and transfer with a Sharpie. If hooking the back side of the cozy, move the Red Dot Tracer over and transfer outline of the cozy.
5. Cut starter strips of wool—black, white, yellow, oatmeal & beige boucle

Hooking for the Front

Start hooking. I started with the soft white and outlined the windows and door. Then the black crosses in the windows and sheep's faces, ears and legs, and the door—outlining them vertically and then filling in. Using the yellow, fill in the windows in a vertical direction, and add a small piece to the door for a handle. Next, I outlined the baby sheep in oatmeal and continued filling in by following the outline. Outline the large sheep in the beige boucle and then fill in hooking in a higgly/piggly style. I was not concerned with the heights here. Give them added texture to their coats with soft white. I hooked two rows to outline the house and for the fence. Use one row on the slates and two rows for the post. Cut your mottled red for the house and charcoal to outline the cozy following its outline. Hook one row all the way around the cozy. Starting at the top of the house, fill in using mottled red, hooking left to right until house is completely filled in. Hook your roof in a vertical direction. Hook your path in a higgly/piggly fashion. Hook your top pasture in the teal/green/brown check. Using a variety of greens hook your front and side grasses in a hit and miss style.

The Back

I appliquéd the back of this cozy, but the back can be hooked if you prefer.

Some ideas for hooking the back are:
- Transfer only the sheep to the bottom and fill in with the check to have sheep grazing in the pasture
- Add a willow tree to the center
- Hit-and-miss style is always a great way to use up those stray strips.

Wooly Saltbox Cozy (front design), 12$\frac{1}{2}$" x 17", #6-cut wool on monk's cloth. A Teresa Kogut Design. Hooked by Kim Kowula, Prim N Proper Stitches, Calgary, Alberta, Canada, 2009.

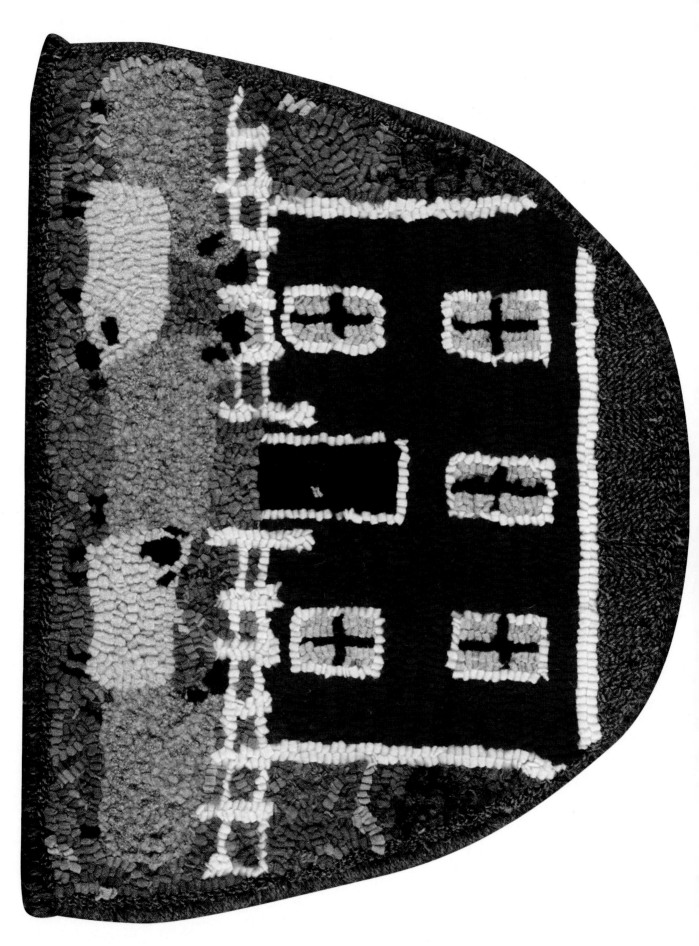

Wooly Saltbox Cozy (back design), 12½" x 1/", wool appliqué on wool backing. A Teresa Kogut Design. Sewn and appliquéd by Kim Kowula, Prim N Proper Stitches, Calgary, Alberta, Canada, 2009.

- Create scallops on the edge and write "W O O L" in the center.

Whatever you decide to do with the back will make it a "one of a kind" tea cozy.

Finishing

We are big whippers up here when it comes to finishing our rugs. We use a bulky 3-ply yarn on the primitive style rugs or a tapestry yarn for finer cuts.

- Begin by marking off a ½" outline around your project. I simply mark of the ½" here and there with a Sharpie and tape measure so I can stay on track when serging. Cut your foundation down to around 1". Serge or zigzag on the ½" outline. Cut down again.

- Starting with the bottom side, fold forward to the outline row of hooking, pin and continue around the top to the other side. Do not do the bottom edge at this point. Repeat for the back.

Materials List

- Fabric: Wool–front only
- Soft white–6" x 16"–house, door & window outline, fence
- Oatmeal–6" x 16"–small sheep
- Beige Boucle–fat ⅛ yard–large sheep
- Dark mottled red–fat ¼ yard–house
- Rust, orange plaid–4" x 16" path
- Mixed greens–fat ⅛ yard–bottom grass
- Teal, green & brown check–4" x 16" top pasture
- Roof & edging–black herringbone–fat ⅛ yard
- Foundation–monk's cloth–20" x 23" (with back 20" x 42")
- Red Dot Tracer
- Sharpie
- Charcoal PNP 3 ply yarn–25 yards for whipping edges & bottom
- Cotton fabric for lining–18" x 45"
- Batting–optional
- Bent Needle for whipping

*Finished size 12½" x 17" before whipping; with whipping 13½" x 17½"

This cozy was hooked in a #6 but lends itself very well to smaller cuts.

Line drawing used for **Wooly Saltbox Cozy.**

Wool samples used for hooking **Wooly Saltbox Cozy.**

Kim Kowula

*Kim Kowula has had a
life long affair with wool,
instilled by her grandmother
and mother. Kim knits,
needlepoints, and appliques
as well as enjoying rug
hooking. In 1981 she started
a business called Simply
Unique Pot Pourri, a.k.a.
Prim N Proper Stitches,
where she vended items
made through her business.
Two years ago, Kim
began operating Prim N
Proper Stitches, a Woolen
Company on the Internet.
She sells wool rovings, hand
dyed yarn, wool fabric,
and rug hooking patterns
from the licensed artwork of
Teresa Kogut. For further
information about Kim
and her company, contact
her web site at www.
primnproperstitches.com.*

- With right sides facing out, line up the front and back. Use the outline rows of your hooking as your guide. Switch pins so you now have them going through both edgings.
- Thread your large eye bent needle (I like the clover gold needle) with about two arm lengths of yarn.
- Starting on the bottom side again, run your needle through the hole next to your outline row, same for back and front, pull your yarn through and move to the next hole to start whipping. Hold about 1" of the end of your yarn on the back edge to secure in place. Continue whipping to the other bottom side. When the need arises to change your yarn, simply thread your needle through your finished whipping for five or six stitches and pull. Cut any extra yarn close to whipping. Start

whipping again only running your yarn through the back completed stitches to hold your end, and continue whipping in the next hole to your outline hooked stitch. You should now have a nice ½ inch high whipping around your cozy with the edging of your foundation acting as cording.

- Whip the bottom of the cozy the same as the sides by folding your foundation to the front and lining up at the first row of hooking.

Complete as above, taking care at the sides by adding an extra whip or two to fill in.

NOTE: *This pattern and all others shown in this book can be ordered through the* **Rug Hooking** *magazine web site at* **www. rughookingmagazine.com.**

General Rug Hooking Instructions

Basic instructions to help you transfer a pattern, finish a rug, and hook with strips of wool

Transferring a Pattern to Backing

Beginning rug hookers often have problems figuring out how to transfer a printed pattern (such as we supply with our Dear Beginning Rug Hooker stories) onto a rug backing (burlap, monk's cloth, etc.). There are several ways to go about it, but the first step in all cases is to decide how big you want your rug to be.

Once you've determined that, a pen, ruler, and a little arithmetic are needed for one transferring method. Draw a grid over the printed pattern. For a simple pattern the grid's squares can be large; for a complex one, make them small. Use the same number of squares to draw a grid on the rug backing. To achieve proper proportions, calculate the size of the squares. Say you want your rug to be a 40" square, and you've used 8 squares across the top of your printed pattern's grid. 40÷8=5, so that means your 8 squares on the backing should be 5" on each side. You also used 8 squares down the side of the pattern, so you'll also use eight, 5" squares along the side as well. This grid will allow you to draw fragments of the pattern in the correct spot and in the correct proportion.

Another method employs a copy machine and nylon veiling (available at fabric stores). After you've used the copier to enlarge the pattern to the desired size, tape the veiling over it and trace all the lines onto the veiling. (It helps to have a transparent ruler to get the lines perfectly straight.) Then tape the marked veiling onto the backing. Retrace the lines on the veiling with a felt-tip pen so they bleed through onto the backing.

An iron-on pattern pencil that makes an indelible blue line can also help you transfer. (The pencils are available through suppliers who advertise in *Rug Hooking*.) Tape tracing paper over the pattern. Using a light table or a sunny window, trace the design onto the tracing paper with an ordinary pencil; turn the tracing paper over and draw over the lines with the pattern pencil, making a mirror image of the design.

Set your iron on high (cotton setting) and allow it to heat up well. Place the tracing paper with the mirror image down on the backing. Holding the paper securely, iron slowly over the design. Press hard, and do not move the iron around the design. Lift and reposition carefully until you have pressed the entire design. Be patient to allow enough time for the lines to be transferred onto the backing. (The pencil lines turn blue as they transfer.)

To check if the pattern has transferred successfully, lift a corner of the paper carefully so that it doesn't move. When all the lines are clearly visible on the burlap, it is ready.

Finish Before You Start

Finishing the edges of hooked pieces is critically important to improve their durability, particularly for floor rugs. When walked on for a number of years, poorly finished edges crack and split, requiring reconstruction that may be unsightly.

Unfortunately, even some experienced rug hookers do not finish their edges well. A quick review of common finishing techniques will benefit even the most seasoned rug hookers and may keep beginners from forming bad habits.

Before you begin hooking a pattern, machine stitch two rows around the perimeter as a defense against fraying. Stitch the first row $1/4$" beyond what will be the hooked portion, and the second row $1/4$" beyond the first row ($1/2$" beyond the hooked portion). Overstitch each row of straight stitches with a row of zigzag stitches as shown in **Figure 1**.

After hooking the entire rug, vacuum it lightly and check it for mistakes. Lay it on a sheet wrong-side up and cover it with a damp towel. Stamp press it lightly with a dry iron to flatten it; do not rub it as if ironing clothing. Rehook bulging or uneven areas before finishing the edges.

The finished edge should be as high as the hooking, so select cording accordingly. Use preshrunk, natural-fiber cording: clothesline, heavy twine, etc.

Fold the backing toward the backside of the rug, about $1/2$" from the hooked portion. Insert the cording and baste it into place with thread as shown in **Figure 2**. When whipped with yarn, the cording preserves the edge of the rug by taking the pressure of footsteps.

Figure 1

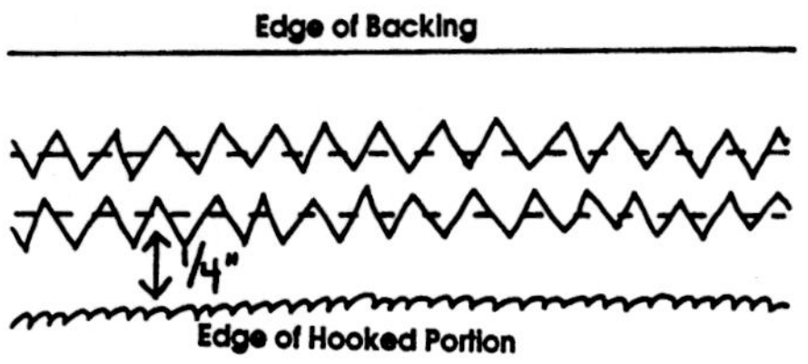

Edge of Backing

$1/4$"

Edge of Hooked Portion

Figure 2

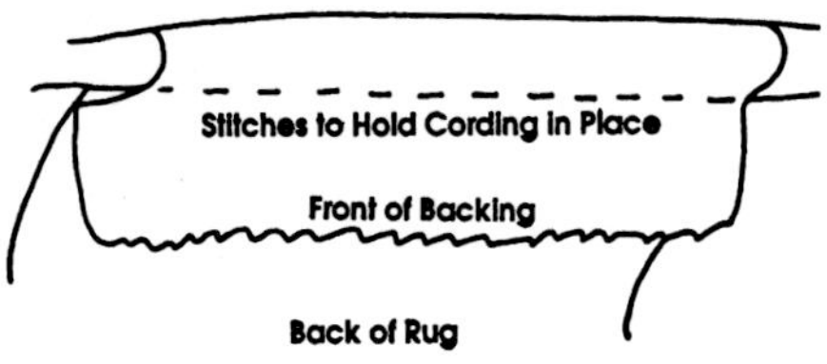

Stitches to Hold Cording in Place

Front of Backing

Back of Rug

Figure 3

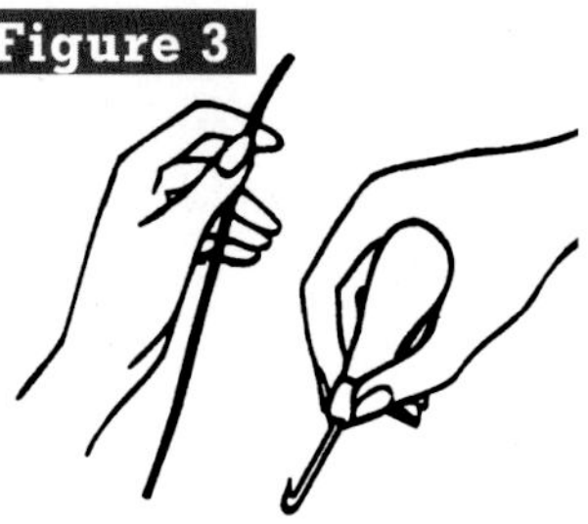

Dye woolen yarn to match your border or to coordinate with your color plan. After the cording is in place, whip the yarn around it with a blunt needle. You will use about one foot of yarn for each inch of whipping.

To whip the edge, simply sew yarn around the cording that is already covered with backing. Whip right up to the edge of the hooked portion on the front, out the back of the rug, around the cording, and down into the front again.

Continue around the perimeter of the rug, making sure the whipping covers the backing evenly. Do not start at a corner. At the corners, you will need to whip more stitches to cover the backing, and you will not be able to create perfectly square corners.

On the backside of the rug, handstitch 1¼" cotton binding tape right up to the edge of the whipping. Miter the tape and the backing at the corners. Cut away the excess backing so the raw edge is hidden under the tape. Finally, sew the inner edge of the tape between loops in the back of the hooked portion to cover the raw edge of the backing.

Sew a label onto the back of your rug. Include your name and location, the name and dimensions of the rug, the designer, the date, and any other pertinent information. Give the rug one final steam press as described above, using a much wetter towel. Lay it flat to dry.

How to Hook

These basic instructions apply to hooking with all widths of woolen strips. Step 3, however, applies to hooking with narrow strips in #3, 4, and 5 cuts. (The number refers to the numerical designation of a cutter wheel on a fabric cutting machine. A #3 wheel cuts a strip ³/₃₂" wide; a #5 cuts a strip ⁵/₃₂" wide; a #8, ⁸/₃₂" or ¼" wide, and so on.) Refer to the section on hooking with wide strips for special tips on holding a hook when making a wide-cut rug.

1. Stretch the backing in a hoop or frame with the design side up. Sitting comfortably, rest the hoop or frame on a table or your lap. The thumbscrew of a hoop should be opposite you.

2. With your left hand (right hand if you're a leftie) hold the end of a woolen strand between your thumb and forefinger (**Figure 3**).

3. With your right hand, hold the hook as if it were a pencil, with your fingertips on the metal collar as shown.

4. Hold the wool in your left hand and put it beneath the backing. With your right hand, push the hook down through the mesh. The shaft of the hook should touch your left forefinger and slide behind

the woolen strip. Push the wool onto the barb with your left thumb.

5. With the hook, pull the end of the strip through to the front of the backing with the hook, to a height of about ½".

6. Push the hook down through the backing a little to the left of the strip's end and catch the strip underneath. Pull up a ⅛" loop, or as high as the strip is wide. To prevent pulling out the previous loop, lean the hook back toward the previous loop as you pull up another loop.

7. Working from right to left, make even loops that gently touch each other as in **Figure 4**. With fine strips, hook in almost every hole. Never put more than one loop in a hole.

8. When you reach the end of the woolen strip, pull the end up through the backing. Pull all ends through to the front as you hook. Tails on the back are untidy and can be easily pulled out.

9. Start the next strip in the same hole in which the last strip ended, again leaving a ½" tail.

10. Trim the ends even with the loops after making several loops with the new strip.

11. Continue the hooking process until the pattern is complete. To keep the back of the rug from becoming lumpy, do not cross a row of hooking with another strip. Cut the strip and start again.

12. Practice the following exercises to achieve the proper rhythm and technique: (a) after hooking straight lines, try wavy lines; (b) pack rows against one another to form a pile as in **Figure 5**.

Even the most skilled rug hooker must pull out loops now and then. Individual strands can be removed easily, but loops in packed areas are harder to remove. Use the hook or a pair of tweezers. Strands may be re-used if they are not badly frayed, and the blank area of the backing may be hooked again.

Hooking with Wide Strips

When hooking with wide strips (¼" to ½"), note that they pull up more easily if you hold the hook in the palm of your hand (**Figure 6**) and insert it into the backing at a sharper angle. (Some even prefer to hold the hook in this manner when working with narrow strips.) As with narrow strips, the shaft of the hook should rub the forefinger of your left hand and pass behind the woolen strip. The barb should hit your thumb, which pushes the wool onto the hook. Never loop the wool over the hook with your left hand; this will result in a lumpy back. If you cannot pick up the strip with your hook, the barb is not properly positioned.—*Happy and Steve DiFranza*

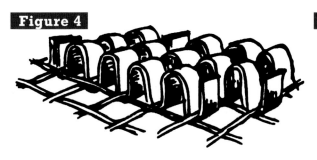

Figure 4

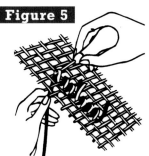

Figure 5

Figure 6

Rug Hooking Resources

Pattern Contributors

The Blue Tulip
Tulip Basket Runner
Karen Worthington
656 Harmony Brass Castle Rd.
Harmony, NJ 08865
908-859-6350
www.thebluetulipwoolery.com
karen@thebluetulipwoolery.com

Crow Hill Primitives
Peaceful Garden
Sharon Soule
4 Westvale Rd.
Kennebunkport, ME 04046
207-967-0573
www.crowhillprimitives.com
info@crowhillprimitives.com

Gene Shepherd
Fowl Mood
108 N. Vine St.
Anaheim, CA 92805
714-956-5150
www.geneshepherd.com
gene@geneshepherd.com

GoingGray
Very Veggie Runner
Martha Reeder and Liz Quebe
3203 Hill Ct. SW
Rochester, MN 55902
507-285-9414
www.goinggray.com
martha@goinggray.com

Hooked Treasures
Abundance
Cherylyn Brubaker
6 Iroquois Circle
Brunswick, ME 04011
207-729-1380
www.hookedtreasures.com
cherylyn@hookedtreasures.com

Mustard Seed Primitives
Sheep's in the Meadow
Marti Taylor and Connie Litfin
5528 W. 62nd St.
Indianapolis, IN 46268
317-387-0052
www.mustardseedprimitive designs.com
mustardseedprimitivedesigns @yahoo.com

Northwoods Wool
Calico Cat Pillow
Jill Holmes
P. O. Box 1027
Cumberland, WI 54829
715-822-3198
www.northwoodswool.com
northwoodswool@yahoo.com

Olde Scotties Primitives
My Primitive Tulip
Lois Roy
63 Lilac Ave.
Woonsocket, RI 02895
401-765-1646
www.oldescottiesprimitives.com
lois@oldescottiesprimitives.com

Payton Primitives
Botanical Garden Sampler
Tina Payton
P. O. Box 40
Mexico, ME 04257
207-364-2172
www.paytonprimitives.com
paytons1@roadrunner.com

Prim n' Proper Stitches
Wooly Saltbox Cozy
Kim Kowula
129 3809 45th St. SW
Calgary, AB T3E 3H4
403-242-7974
www.primnproperstitches.com
simplyunique@shaw.ca

The Red Saltbox
Sheep Sampler
Wendy Miller
The Robinson House
503 S. Brady St.
Attica, IN 47918
765-762-6292
www.theredsaltbox.com
theredsaltbox@yahoo.com

Rittermere-Hurst-Field
Sherman
Jeanne Field
P. O. Box 487
Aurora, ON L4G 3L6
800-268-9813
www.LetsHookRugs.com
rhf@letshookrugs.com

Rug Art and Supply/Threads of Comfort Designs
Snow Day
Shelley Flannery and
Barbara Hanson
3037 NE Brogden
Hillsboro, OR 97124
503-648-3979
www.rugartsupply.com
shelley-barbara@rugartsupply.com

Spruce Ridge Studio
Under the Willow
Kris Miller
1786 Eager Rd.
Howell, MI 48855
517-546-7732
www.spruceridgestudios.com
kris@spruceridgestudios.com

Star Rug Company
Bird Rug
Maria Barton
6191 Link Drive
Indian River, MI 49749
231-238-6894
www.starrugcompany.com
starrugcompany@freeway.net

Additional Rug Hooking Suppliers

American Folk Art and Craft Supply
Michele Stenson
1415 Hanover St., Rte. 139
Hanover, MA 02339
781-871-7288
www.americanfolkartonline.com
Over 100 hand-dyed colors, rug hooking and braiding supplies

Angel Girl A Rug Hooking Studio
Victoria Jacobson
321 S. Main St.
Stillwater, MN 55082
612-741-2529
www.angelgirlstudio.com
Wool, classes, gifts, supplies and more

Bolivar Cutters
Joan Bolivar
P. O. Box 539
Bridgewater, NS B4V 2X6
902-543-7762
www.bolivarcutter.com
Cutting machines

Cat House Rugs
Jyl Clark
415 W. First St.
New Albany, IN 47150
812-945-RUGS
www.cathouserugs.com
Supplies, wool, patterns, kits, featuring Kaye Miller Designs

Emma Lou's Primitives
Emma Lou Lais
20614 W. 47th St.
Shawnee, KS 66218
913-745-5605
www.emmalousprimitives.com
Primitive rug patterns

Green Mountain Hooked Rugs, Inc.
Stephanie Ashworth-Krauss
2838 County Rd.
Montpelier, VT 05602
802-485-7274
www.GreenMountainHooked Rugs.com
Patterns, supplies, and the annual Green Mountain Rug School

Halcyon Yarn
12 School St.
Bath, ME 04530
800-341-0282
www.halcyonyarn.com
High quality rug yarn for finishing hooked rugs

Heavens to Betsy
Betsy Reed
46 Route 23
Claverack, NY 12513
www.heavens-to-betsy.com
Milled wool for rug hooking, penny rugs, applique, quilting and more.

Hook Nook
Margaret Lutz
49 Samson Drive
Flemington, NJ 08822
908-806-8083
www.hook-nook.com
Lib Callaway rug patterns, hooking supplies and instructions

L.J. Fibers
Laurie Lausen
4750 Grand Ave. S.
Minneapolis, MN 55419
www.ljfibers.com
Kits, wool, patterns, supplies, books, classes and events

Liziana Creations
Diana O'Brien
P. O. Box 310
Shelburne, MA 01370
www.liziana.com
Supplies, backings, books, kits, wool, patterns, designs, and more

Moondance Color Company
622 Spencer Rd.
Oakham, MA 01068
508-882-3383
www.moondancecolor.com
Woolen fabrics, threads, patterns and kits

Primitive Spirit
Karen Kahle
P. O. Box 1363
Eugene, OR 97440
541-344-4316
www.primitivespiritrugs.com
Patterns, dye books, dvds, catalogs

Spruce Top Rug Hooking Studio
Carol Harvey-Clark
255 W. Main St.
Mahone Bay, NS B0J 2E0
888-RUG-HOOK
www.sprucetoprughooking studio.com

The Wool Basket
Karen Haskett
526 N. Cleveland Ave.
Loveland, CO 80537
970-203-0999
www.thewoolbasket.com

The Wool Studio
Rebecca Erb
706 Brownsville Rd.
Sinking Spring, PA 19608
610-678-5448
www.thewoolstudio.com
Quality woolens, specializing in textures for the primitive rug hooker

Townsend Industries, Inc.
P. O. Box 97
Altoona, IA 50009
877-868-3544
www.townsendindustries.com
Fabric cutters, frames

W. Cushing and Company
21 North St., Box 351
Kennebunkport, ME 04046
207-967-3711
www.wcushing.com
Joan Moshimer's rug hooking studio, Cushing Perfection dyes, Pearl McGown patterns, rug hooking supplies

Whispering Hill Farm
Donna Swanson
Box 186, Rte. 169
S. Woodstock, CT 06267
860-928-0162
www.whispering-hill.com
Complete rug hooking supplier: wool, hooks, patterns, backings, books, frames, cutters.